P9-AFN-122

# Life Is a Dream

# Life Is a Dream

## A Play by Pedro Calderón de la Barca

Translated and with a Foreword
and Introduction by Edwin Honig

A MERMAID DRAMABOOK
Hill & Wang   *New York*

And there's *Life Is a Dream*!
The stage for the play is always set, the lights
always lit, the actors,
forever the same, ardently speak their lines,
go out and come back,
resuming their roles, repeating their lines, twenty-four
hours a day.
It's the world's best unfinished play, ending only to start
all over again
without any break. And the beauty of it—what makes it
all click—is this:
you can take all the roles, sitting back in your mind's
dark theatre to watch,
no matter when you came in. The bewildered girl,
who greets you at first,
is dressed as a man (and is mistaken as such
until the end
by all but her flunkey, the clown, who dies oddly biting
his martyred tongue)—
poor thing, she's out for the blood of the playboy duke,
who betrayed her once,
but then mismarries her after all; or the wild
young father-devouring
Prince, who all but digests his meal on the stage
and makes you enjoy it;
or the half-eaten King himself, who's losing his grip
(the old story)
and pretends it's the fault of his slavishly loyal psychiatrist
oracle, who
it's plain the King was always too bright to believe.
The message, of course
(says the play going on), is *Long live the King of Life!*
whoever he is.

E.H.

# Contents

# Foreword

## *The Playwright*

THE EMINENCE of Pedro Calderón de la Barca (1600–1681) in Spanish drama is equaled only by that of Lope de Vega (1562–1635). Calderón wrote over two hundred works for the theatre: nearly one hundred twenty full-length plays, eighty *autos sacramentales* (a type of one-act morality play he brought to perfection), and a miscellaneous score of *entremeses* (interludes) and short dramatic pieces. Lope, who wrote at least seven times as many plays, is proverbially known as "the monster of nature" while Calderón's equivalent title is "the monster of ingenuity."

Born into a prominent Castilian family in Madrid—his father being Secretary to the Council of the Treasury—Calderón was educated by the Jesuits, studied law at Salamanca, rhetoric and logic at Alcalá, and was complimented by Lope de Vega in 1620 for some verses written especially for the canonization of San Isidro, patron saint of Madrid. Made a Knight of Santiago in 1637, he served as a soldier from 1638 to 1642 and became a priest in 1651. Three Spanish monarchs favored him, and many of his plays, including those commissioned by the Court, were acknowledged the best dramatic work of his time. Besides Lope his contemporaries included Cervantes, Velásquez, Murillo, Gracián, Quevedo, Tirso de Molina, and Góngora—the most celebrated artists and writers of the Golden Age.

A French diplomat, reporting a conversation with the old playwright in 1669, concluded that Calderón knew next to nothing generally, and perhaps least of all about the rules of drama, which he mocked. Calderón is said to have died while writing a new play.

## The Play

*La vida es sueño* (1635/6) is his best-known play, and also the most universally celebrated in the history of the Spanish theatre. Its main theme, the transience of human life, an- cient as man himself, is still proverbial in the schoolchil- dren's round which ends, "Life is but a dream." Fascinated scholars have traced the theme to earliest Oriental philoso- phy and religion, to the Taoist ethic and Buddhist thought, to appropriate passages in Job, Isaiah, and Ecclesiastes, to Heraclitus, Plato, and Roman Stoicism, and finally to Chris- tian ethics and apologetics—the tradition closest to Cal- derón's thinking as a deeply religious seventeenth-century man in a militant Catholic country whose empire had begun to dissolve.

Besides the subject of life's ephemerality, the play employs at least three other traditional ideas and motifs: the myth of the hero as a lost or sequestered child, the legend of the drugged and transported sleeper, and the idea of man over- coming the auguries of fate proposed through an adverse reading of the stars. Professor A. E. Sloman has recently shown that the most important source for the play is an- other play written the previous year by Calderón himself in collaboration with Antonio Coello, *Yerros de naturaleza y aciertos de la fortuna* (1634)—*Nature's Errors Redeemed by Fortune*. Studies of the relationship between these two plays should permit new insights into the workings of Calderón's creative imagination.

The first publication of *La vida es sueño* was edited by Don Joseph Calderón, the playwright's brother, who put it at the head of a collection of twelve plays in *Primera parte de comedias de Don Pedro Calderón de la Barca* . . . (1636). Another, though defective, edition appeared in an anthology published the same year in Zaragoza. Two further editions of Don Joseph's collection appeared in 1640; a spurious printing was put out by another editor around 1670; and still another (from which most Spanish texts of the play have since been derived) appeared in 1685, also entitled *Primera parte* and edited by Don Juan de Vera Tassis y Villaroel, who claimed the title of "best friend" to Don Pedro. The best modern editions of the play are by Professor A. E. Sloman (Manchester, 1961) and by Professor E. E. Hesse (New York, 1961).

Before our age of scholarly books and articles, the surest index to a literary work's readability was the foreign adaptations and translations it received. Ángel Valbuena Briones, in his *Perspectiva critica* . . . (Madrid, 1965), lists five such seventeenth-century appearances, including one in Dutch and one in Italian during the year of the play's first publication, 1636. Another Dutch translation appeared in 1647, and a second Italian one in 1664. The score and libretto of a German opera based on the play were printed in Hamburg in 1693. Several French and further Italian versions appeared in the early eighteenth century; but from then until about 1870 more than seventeen German adaptations, operas, and translations came into existence, confirming the fact that Calderón's *Life Is a Dream* was most popular in the country where Romanticism first reared its head in Europe. The first translation in English (by Malcolm Cowan) appeared in 1830, and an early Russian one in 1861.

Until recently the play in English translation was best known through Edward Fitzgerald's wildly free adaptation; its main virtue over the other and much "closer" nineteenth-century version by Reverend Denis F. MacCarthy is that Fitzgerald's is readable. Among half a dozen contemporary translations are two by English poets, Roy Campbell (in *The Classic Theatre, III,* ed. E. Bentley, New York, 1959) and Kathleen Raine (London, 1968).

## The Translation and the Original

THERE IS A PREVAILING TREND to translate seventeenth-century Spanish and French plays into English blank verse and pseudo-Elizabethan diction. Even when a poet as good as Roy Campbell does it, the result can be disappointing, a bit like overstretching a nice, thick, red rubber band till it is cracked and limp. The regular iambic beat, the jogging rhetoric and finessed periphrases are not comparable to the verbal and metrical patterns of the Spanish original. Calderón's diction is generally plain, if not always direct. There are inversions and frills but in especially designated places. What distinguishes his particular idiom are, first, the variety of verse forms and rhyme patterns, which must be exact because they are traditional and expected;* second, a standard kind of imagery or trope system stressing the symmetrical balance of argument, and partly derived from Góngora's so-called conceptist style; third, long soliloquies which are meant to identify the speaker through his characteristic situation. The sense of this usage is that what a man *says*—the

* The practice initiated by Lope de Vega is to use a variety of meters and lines for special effects that coincide with the engagements and shifts of character and action in a verse play. Calderón follows Lope in this practice, and in *Life Is a Dream* he employs six typical measures: *silva, décima, romance, quintilla, redondilla, octava.*

The *silva* is made up of rhymed couplets with alternating lines of seven and eleven syllables; the tone is lyric and the measure can be used for dialogue. In this play *silvas* occur only in the three scenes where Rosaura and Segismundo appear together. The *décima*, as the term implies, is a ten-line stanzaic form in irregularly rhymed patterns; it is reserved for speeches involving complaints or arguments, and is used here only for significant soliloquies by Segismundo. *Romance*, the commonest measure, used mainly for narration, is based on an eight-syllable line with assonantal rhymes of alternating vowels, as in this play, A-E, I-O, E-A, E-E, E-O, O-A, and A-A. The *quintilla*, like the *décima*, is framed on set line-units; its five lines are octosyllabic but only two lines may rhyme, and no three consecutively. The measure is used for complimentary dialogues. The *redondilla* is a quatrain form of octosyllabic lines rhyming *abba* and employed to incorporate fast-moving dramatic action. *Octavas* are eight-line octosyllabic units, used to mark off portentous events or speeches; the lines rhyme *abababcc*, like a little sonnet.

things he reasons about and quarrels with—identifies him rather than what he does. What he does issues from what he thinks he must be, an instrument of fate—"a representable idea," as Entwistle calls it—which activates his dramatic role. What he does, then, is ritualized according to his role, his duty, his status in the play. In this he goes through his paces like a company of *toreros*—charged with fighting bulls according to prescribed stages or *acts*—until like the matador in the dénouement he delivers the *coup de grâce*.

Not only are the characters ritualized but the plots in their complications may also be considered exemplifications of fate. Plot intrigue calls for long soliloquies, set speeches, as well as quick exchanges, expletives, and outcries, all more or less conventionalized. And these aspects of the play have more to do with expected implications of the theme—honor impasse, insult, revenge motif, siege of jealousy, personal anxiety—than with any simple determinism of a psychological kind. (This is perhaps why Calderón is closer in feeling to Jonson and Racine—court dramatists, masque writers—than to Shakespeare or to any other English or French contemporary.)

Like the plot, the language in *Life Is a Dream* is formal and stylized; yet it is not as complex as the language of *Hamlet*; it can be understood by third-year college students of Spanish. There are complexities in sentence structure, diction, and imagery, but all in predictable sequences. Like a many-petaled rose, they open just enough to let the curious fragrance out. The rose stays relatively tight throughout. In spite of such limitations there is real eloquence (as in the exchanges between Segismundo and his father, the King) and several instances of magniloquence. Both kinds of linguistic virtuosity occur in soliloquies and stand out like statues jutting up bare and proud among the trimmed hedgerows in a formal park.

Calderón's vocabulary is not extensive; it does not begin to compare with the exuberant inventiveness of Shakespeare's or Jonson's. But though limited, it is precise; in line with thematic progression its use of synonyms for aspects of good and bad luck is almost obsessive and repetitious. There are also frequent locutions for the idea and imagery of honor, reputation, identity, and a curiously symmetrical design for the metaphoric presentation of the typical state of mind called *turbación*—anxiety, the cousin to melancholy.

Formal relationships follow the rule of characterization. They are framed according to a dominant trait and made to exemplify the chief thematic concern through the language of courteous exchange, flowery speeches, aria-like dialogues, obedient replies, closely reasoned soliloquies—and all expressly demonstrating fixed patterns of social behavior: daughter to father, father to son, vassal to king, and so forth. Since the claims of honor and pride override other considerations, and since the threat of sexual assault is always imminent, there is little chance for a genuine relationship between man and woman to develop. Love always appears to be tortured, aborted, frightened out of its wits. The laws of society stand implacable at the center and outside the gates whirl the offended and the victimized isolatos.

The soliloquy and the set speech typify such conditions and relationships. For the one is as much a result of pressured thought which cannot otherwise be communicated as the other is cultivated rhetorical clothing of depersonalized class behavior. Both are extreme expressions, and neither speaks for the real individual who is trying to emerge from behind the conventions. The only way he can begin to emerge is through exercising his appointed role as a high or low character. Suitable to each character in the play, therefore, are both the social language of his class and the personal language of his feelings. Depending on the occasion, a character may be expected to speak either the standard language befitting his role and function among his fellow men or the more particular speech expressing his wit, passion, sense of revelation, or self-discovery. It is of course the purpose of the various types of verse measures to help emphasize such shifts and differences.

For this translation I have adopted the simplified metrical contrivance employed in my translations of *Calderón: Four Plays* (Hill and Wang, New York, 1961) and explained in the introduction to that volume:

"I use a syllabic line, patterned on the octosyllabic *romance*, but differing from its model (which sometimes omits and sometimes adds a syllable) in permitting a regular six-to-nine-syllable limitation. The advantage of such flexibility is that the basic syllabic quantity allows for a fairly regular accentual beat to emerge in a variety of trimeter, tetrameter, and pentameter lines that is not foreign to the English ear, and yet is just strange enough to suggest the Spanish norm. . . . If someone objects that the lines too often read like maladjusted prose, I would point out that there is the same effect in the original when prose diction is cast in verse simply to abide by Golden Age conventions in this regard. It would have been futile to follow such usages when what I was trying mainly to do was reflect the essential poetry of Calderón's language as well as stick to its prose sense. But if, as I hope, [this version of the play is] dramatically acceptable to readers whom the insipidities of verbal compromise, archaisms, and double-headed anachronisms normally discourage, then I will have succeeded in delivering the substance, and hence some of the strange raw flavor, of the thing in the original."

EDWIN HONIG

# The Magnanimous Prince:
## *Life Is a Dream*

THE APPEAL OF *Life Is a Dream* can never be wholly accounted for. From one point of view it seems incomplete, even fragmentary, like Marlowe's *Doctor Faustus*. From another, the play powerfully condenses in its enacted metaphor of living-and-dreaming an overwhelming perception about life's worth together with man's failure to make much of it. The play is many-faceted: it keeps changing as one holds it up to scrutiny so that its real theme seems impossible to pin down. It has the appeal of a mystery, but one in which the living energy that makes up the mystery is withheld, and while being withheld gets transformed into something different from the rigid terms and structure meant to contain it. Though following a straightforward dramatic pattern and the clearly stated and often repeated idea framed in the title, the play's meanings are not reducible, as they are often made to seem, to a few neat exempla about the turnings of fate and religious belief. The meanings grow, they shift their ground, they multiply with each reading. It is what happens in all great literary works: for a moment we behold the full and clear design only to note immediately beneath it the baffling multiplicity of effects raying out beyond into so many intimately related ideas we cannot even begin to name them.*

In this play honor is seen in its broadest possible sense as related to the whole of life, interwoven with the very substance and meaning of life. The title implies the question, Is life worth living? By a further implication, if honor is an illusion, so is life, and if this is true, how does one cope with such a vast and fearful discovery?

Another related and basic problem is the question of how to deal with the violent and secret crimes of the older generation. Since Rosaura as well as Segismundo have been dishonored by their fathers, how can they redress their personal grievances without rupturing the relationship of one generation with the next, the succession of life itself? The old myths stir beneath the surface: Zeus dethroned

---

* Suggestive of such complexity are two observations of Professor Entwistle's made, however, about another Calderón play, *Devotion to the Cross*.

> The evidence of the senses is not denied, but it is checked and corrected. The world of phenomena is, admittedly, a dream, but there is a network of realities immediately underneath the surface and embracing the correlated postulates of all the sciences. It is this world which Calderón reveals in a number of his great plays.

Accordingly, Entwistle sees that *Devotion to the Cross*

> is, like any of the *autos*, a representable idea. The characters are individual exponents of leading principles. They are seen, so to speak, beneath the epidermis, in their essential structure. As infrared photographs eliminate the superficial differentiae without confounding different individuals, so Calderón's actors lose something of the personality conferred by a thousand superficial details without ceasing to be individual entities. (William J. Entwistle, "Calderón et le théatre symbolique," *Bulletin Hispanique*, LII [1950], 41–54.)

One can apply these observations to *Life Is a Dream*. The first, in pointing to Calderón's moral realism, leads to one definition of the theme—the triumph of consciousness in experience—in a play which is dramatically formed by a series of actions and soliloquies imitating a dream vision. The second observation, about the subcutaneous nature of the moral life, leads one to look for the life of impulse, which when followed even superficially in this play tells a good deal about the intricate emotional dynamics that make it such an absorbing document of psychological realism.

Cronus (as Calderón fully showed in another play, *La estatua de Prometeo—Prometheus' Statue*); Zeus raped Leda as a swan and Europa as a bull; Aeneas abandoned Dido. All the actions pertain here to the sexual crimes of worldly men as fathers and lovers. Clotaldo raped and abandoned Violante, Rosaura's mother, and the rapist duke Astolfo abandoned Rosaura. In political terms, Segismundo will swear to overcome his father and trample on his beard.

Rosaura and Segismundo both have good cause to seek vengeance. They have been brutalized. Rosaura has been raped, deprived of her sexual honor, and rejected as a woman, without explanation. And, as far as he knows, also without explanation, Segismundo has been spiritually assaulted, deprived of his liberty, his free will, his honor as a man, and left since birth in a prison tower, like his father's guilty rotting dream. Deprived of his power as a man and as a prince, Segismundo has also been left ignorant of the existence of women, of love, of social communion.

To regain her honor (since there is no one to act for her), Rosaura must pretend to be a man—dress and act like one—so that she may have the sexual and political freedom needed to force the issue. To redress his grievances, Segismundo must seek power by revolution, imitate a tyrant in order to dethrone one, so that when he triumphs he can accomplish three things: rectify the misuse of power and dispense justice; restore his own freedom and gain the power proper to him as a man and as a prince; destroy the opposing vision: his father's self-rotting dream.

No other course is possible since, as the situation of the play proposes, even if *la vida es sueño, vida infama no es vida—a life disgraced is no life at all.*

Segismundo must be twice awakened and have Rosaura's help before he attains to consciousness. So too Rosaura, in order to restore her honor as a woman, cannot finally act as a man; when her father fails her she can only seek Segismundo's help. He in turn is thus forced to confront her as a libidinous object and then to recognize that if he were to overmaster and take her as a woman, the act would be a violation of the sort she is now doubly seeking to redress: her father's rape and abandonment of her mother and Astolfo's rape and abandonment of her. She must serve Segismundo as a benign influence, a test and a guide, not as his sexual partner.

Theirs is a strange relationship. It seems that the similarity and common urgency of their grievances have set up something like an incest barrier between them. Perhaps it is not so much a relationship as a brief series of crucial confrontations. She arrives to bring him a new sense of the world of which he has been deprived since birth. Her beauty and her light are essentialized in her name: the spirit of the rose (*rose aura*) and a series of dawns (*auroras*, her name anagrammed). Beholding her beauty and person as the gifts they are, he instinctively wishes to possess them. He must learn that he can have her only as one who identifies his life's struggle for him and as someone who then must share a mission with him. In the darkness of the prison tower, in the open doorway waiting to emit him, Rosaura sees the womb and tomb of life:

> The front door
> stands open to . . . what is it,
> a mausoleum? And pitch darkness
> comes crawling out as though
> the night itself were born inside.

It is life, unaware of itself as yet, for it has been buried in death, a light in the darkness at first, followed by the clanking of chains as the prisoner, man himself, emerges in animal pelts. Can it be that Rosaura is privileged to witness this birth scene because she is Segismundo's "twin"—that at this moment she too is being "born" into consciousness through her recognition of his birth?

We know that Calderón was co-author, with Antonio

Coello, of a *Vida*-like play, *Yerros de naturaleza y aciertos de fortuna—Nature's Errors Redeemed by Fortune,*\* written presumably the year before *La vida es sueño.* The two plays have a good deal in common. The plots are similar, and the names of two characters, Segismundo and Rosaura, identical, though these do not happen to be principal characters in *Yerros.* The leading characters in *Yerros* are an attractive but fatally disrupted set of twins, Matilde and Polidoro, heirs to the throne left vacant by their recently deceased father, King Conrado. Matilde, the daughter, is more aggressive than her brother. In order to gain the throne she plans to kill him (first giving out that she herself has been drowned), then take over his identity and dress and rule in his place. She is aided in the plot by the support of an older (and Clotaldo-like) character, Filipo, who has found Polidoro compromising his daughter Rosaura by entering her room. But instead of doing away with Polidoro, as he has promised, Filipo shuts him up in a tower. Then Segismundo, Filipo's son (Segismundo and Rosaura are indeed brother and sister in *Yerros*), arrives, seeking vengeance on Polidoro, gets into the palace, and kills someone who looks like his intended victim. (The someone of course turns out to be Matilde.) Subsequently Polidoro is brought from the tower and proclaimed king, whereupon he pardons all his enemies and takes Rosaura as his wife.

The unconscious vibrations of attraction and repulsion marking Segismundo's encounters with Rosaura in *Life Is a Dream* seem to have a start in the two sets of sibling relationships (Matilde-Polidoro and Segismundo-Rosaura) in the *Yerros* play. It is almost as if Calderón had not yet brushed out of his mind certain aspects of these relationships—the twins, the masculine sister, the names of other

\* See Albert E. Sloman's excellent discussion of the two plays in Chapter X of his book, *The Dramatic Craftsmanship of Calderón* (Oxford, 1958).

xxi

characters who are related as brother and sister, the incest threat, the accession of the imprisoned man to the kingship at the end—before he began to write the *Vida* play. Vibrations of attraction and repulsion based on the incest taboo are actually featured in other Calderón plays—*Devotion to the Cross* and *The Hair of Absalom*—in which the incest barrier is dramatically broken down. There is a precedent, then, for magnifying such sexual affinities in Calderón. In any case, one reason to stress the unconscious motif here is that the strong cause which Segismundo shares with Rosaura against brutalization is usually scanted in favor of discussions about techniques and metaphysics in the play. It is not often seen that the mysterious interdependence between Rosaura and Segismundo has directly to do with the moral realism of their claims in a male-dominated, autocratic society. They need each other not only to regain their womanhood and manhood, respectively, but also because what they have to face is an extremely adverse and unpromising set of circumstances, not least because they are going against the rule of custom and law as represented by guilty, well-meaning, and unjust men: Basilio, the King; Clotaldo, his chief counselor and Rosaura's father; and Astolfo, the duke. And so the act of restoring the human integer of magnanimity in the face of its thorough brutalization by well-intentioned, civilized men is nothing short of saintly. And this is what Segismundo proceeds to do.

If the life of consciousness is the only life worth living, then Segismundo is clearly the only character in the play who succeeds in attaining it. He emerges from the dream of life, which is the condition of all the other characters, to triumph over the sleep of death, the anonymity in which he is seen at the beginning. The other characters are there to aid, block, and test him along the way, as in a dream vision. Their special counsel is against action, for they use the formula of life-is-a-dream in the narrowest sense, as a palliative, in order to advise, taunt, and even to torment (read *tame*) the prince. But Segismundo's only chance to achieve his own identity is by recognizing that the formula refers to his unborn condition. This he must discover before he can be regenerated.

The stages of his regeneration are marked off by certain of his speeches and soliloquies which other characters overhear, and by actions which they then witness. But the characters, often like figures in a dream, do little or nothing to react further to his behavior in any personal way through the narrative sequence of the play. Through his soliloquies and what he says to others, Segismundo seems constantly to be setting up rationales for acting the way he does as he goes along. The other characters, Rosaura especially, are there to feed him with the possibilities of experience, which will turn out, when he understands it, to confirm his own gradual acquisition of moral consciousness. This sort of procedure, involving both being-there and not-being-there at the same time, resembles what happens in dreams and in dream allegories. There is an unalterable line to be followed which only the consciousness of a single actor may pursue, since it is essentially from his actions leading to his awareness that the real business of the play takes its meanings.

The ambiguous creature wearing animal pelts and lying chained in the tower is the prince of mankind. This is how Segismundo begins. Thereafter we are obliged to judge the moral and psychological distance he traverses in the course of the play in order to become consciously human. He must go from the lowest form of human life, the equivalent of the cave man, to the highest—the human being who learns to be civilized by responding to everything around him while doubting it all and believing in nothing. (How could someone who has scarcely even been born believe in anything?) Others may say life is a dream; Segismundo must find out whether this is true or not by living his own life. He must fight for the power he has been denied, but once it is achieved he must also wear it lightly, pardoning his enemies and renouncing his love. Shakespeare thought of magnanimity in this way too: "They that have the power to hurt and will do none / . . . They are the lords and owners of their faces, / Others but stewards of their excellence." And Donne, of course, too, in lines just as familiar: "Because such fingers need to knit / That subtile knot, which makes us man: / So must pure lovers soules descend / T'affections, and to faculties, / Which sense may reach and apprehend, / Else a great Prince in prison lies."

The precise virtue, then, which Segismundo will attain is magnanimity, the quality of the highest civilized behavior. Battle in a just cause, the pursuit of one's honor, the achievement of knowledge and intellectual pride, and the unswerving course of loyalty are other virtues embodied by characters in the play. But none of these saves them from suffering desperation, an unresolved moral dilemma. Only Segismundo's attainment frees the others; or—since they frequently seem to be little more than figures revolving in Segismundo's orbit—enables the lesser virtues they represent to be seen against his fundamental moral evolution.

Like honor, of which it is part, his magnanimity means nothing in itself; it must be won by experience, past which, as he himself says,

> If my valor is destined
> for great victories, the greatest
> must be the one I now achieve
> by conquering myself.

This is no mere rephrasing of the familiar Greek adage; coming nearly at the end of the play, the sentence rings out as a momentous renunciation of power politics, the life of tooth and claw, the deceptions of intellectual and sexual pride, the blandishments of romantic appetite, and even the ambiguities of filial piety. We see that to achieve magnanimity Segismundo has had fully to recognize who and what he is, through a series of acts which includes one murder and several attempts at murder as well as threats of parricide and rape. He has had to learn to love and then to undo his love, to overcome himself, and to vanquish his father. It is not an easy formula at all. His career is a paradigm of several millennia of human history.

For magnanimity to arise it must contend with the brute in man as well as the brute in society. Half man and half beast as Segismundo recognizes himself to be at the beginning, his first understanding is that though he has an intellect which makes him superior to animals, he lacks the freedom to use it, a freedom which even the animals have.

> A brute is born, its hide all covered
> in brightly painted motley,
> which, thanks to nature's brush, is lovely
> as the sky in star-strewn panoply,
> till learning man's cruel need
> to lunge and pounce on prey
> when it becomes a monster
> in a labyrinth. Then why should I,
> with instincts higher than a brute's,
> enjoy less liberty?

Included in his recognition here are both the labyrinth myth of Theseus and the Minotaur (of which his own present state of being is another version), the interiorized beast in man, and "man's cruel need" to hunt and to imprison a being as natural as himself. His first impulse on having been overheard by Rosaura is to want to kill her for thus learning about his defects: "so you won't know that I know/ you already know my weaknesses." The effect of her plea for compassion—"I throw myself at your feet./ If you were born human,/ my doing so would free me."— is to becalm him: "it is you, and you/alone, who douse the fire of my wrath,/ fill my sight with wonder/ and my hearing with admiration." Apparently the humane virtue is even more powerful than the beast in him. Moreover, in his delight at seeing her and recognizing something about the nature of his needs, he makes a complicated compliment contain a deep psychological truth; for, as he puts it, the prospect of not looking at her now,

> would be worse
> than fiercest death, madness,
> rage, and overwhelming grief.
> It would be life—for, as
> I've had so bitterly to learn,
> bringing life to one who's desperate
> is the same as taking life away
> from one who swims in happiness.

Having just entered Poland, dressed as a man to seek vengeance on Astolfo, Rosaura, a stranger and in misery, is momentarily buoyed up by Segismundo's view of her. It stimulates the civilizing role she is to play from that moment on. Much later, toward the end of the play, Rosaura is to face Segismundo and remind him of the three disguises she has worn in her successive confrontations with him. With each appearance in a different guise she has affected him strongly and unaccountably. He himself tells her that she is like the gift of life to him, who is perhaps dead, perhaps not yet born. She serves to curb his rage, fill him with the sense of wonder, the first stirrings of love for and need for communion with a fellow creature; and she gives him his first taste of inner freedom, the beginning of the conscious life, the sense of self. Even later, when Segismundo is taunted by the doubts and delusions of others, which throw him off, and he wants to take her as a woman in order to escape his fear, we recognize that she also proves her validity as a taboo object—someone with whom he has identified himself too closely, almost incestuously. Much as Julia, Eusebio's actual twin sister,

serves him in *Devotion to the Cross,* Rosaura serves Segismundo as a temptation within him, as a surrogate sister
whom he attempts to violate, as if to challenge or escape
the delusion that if life is merely a dream, he may have no
identity or potency as a man.

Of course in her own right Rosaura is also a victim of
passion. Her first arrival on the scene, which begins the
play, echoes with the wild animal sounds of the horse which
has just thrown her: "mad horse, / half griffin?—You rage
like a storm, / then flicker like lightning outspeeding light,
. . . to hurl / and drag yourself through / this labyrinth of
tangled rocks!" She is a refugee from passion, which partly
explains why she is there, dressed as a man. In the last
act, when she enters on the battlefield to join Segismundo
and to plead for his aid in her personal cause, she is
described as entering "in the loose blouse and wide skirts
of a peasant woman, and wearing a sword and a dagger."
She is both hunter and hunted—the hysterical state of
many a wronged victim of the honor plays. And she suffers
from the ambivalences of her role or successively alternating
roles, suggesting that until she is fully met and honored as
a woman she may be mistaken as an hermaphrodite; the
very ambivalence is a factor here with which Calderón plays:

> As a woman I come hoping to win you
> over to my honor's cause;
> but also as a man would, I come
> to swell your heart, battling for your crown.
> The woman yearning for your sympathy
> kneels down here at your feet;
> the man who comes offering his service
> lends you both his person and his sword.
> But should you turn to take
> the woman in me as all woman,
> the man in me would kill you,
> in strict defense of my good name;
> for, to triumph in the war of love,

> I must be both the humbled woman
> who appeals to you and the man
> who's out for honor and for glory.

Segismundo turns aside and when he finally replies, it is with the full passion of a man who has recognized her as a woman he cannot have:

> I do not even look at you because,
> as someone sworn to look after
> your honor, I have all I can do
> to keep from looking at your beauty.

And Segismundo leaves to join the wild mobs that have put themselves in his hands so that he may seize the kingship.

But we do not leave Rosaura without recalling how much she has served, both consciously and unconsciously, in the play as a civilizing agent. When she needs to appear at court in order to contact Astolfo, she disguises herself as a maid in the service of Estrella, and calls herself Astrea. Then we recognize that the names of mistress and maid here are homonymic and that both names are synonyms for *star*. Estrella is associated more with the idea of fate and destiny (which is what she serves when she becomes Segismundo's wife at the end); Astrea suggests the generic term for *star*. This difference is perhaps contained in another distinction, one which Rosaura herself makes when addressing Astolfo while still disguised as Astrea:

> Es que Estrella—que lo puede
> ser de Venus—me mandó

"[I can only tell you] that Estrella, bright and beautiful/ as Venus, has asked me . . ." There follows the business of the return of the true portrait, which Astolfo is wearing around his neck, demanded by Estrella, and the confusion over two portraits, when there is only one, brought on by Rosaura-Astrea's ruse to get her own back. One wonders if by this interchange Calderón means that Astrea (Rosaura), as the true intended for Astolfo, must first merge with another "star" (Estrella) in disguise before she can claim him, and hence the confusion over (fusion with) the identity of the woman in the disputed portrait. Rosaura, at any rate, succeeds so well with her ruse that she not only recovers her own portrait but also manages to get from Estrella the admission that it—because it looks like Rosaura—is the true one. Incidental to all this, but by no means unimportant, Rosaura has begun to regain her honor.

The analogue to Rosaura's retrieval of her portrait is Segismundo's recognition, almost coincidentally at the end of Act Two, that the relationship between dream and reality, illusion and life, sleeping and waking, might be the same as the imposition of one's free will upon the stream of life, which we call experience:

> for the world
> we live in is so curious
> that to live is but to dream.
> And all that's happened to me tells me
> that while he lives man dreams
> what he is until he wakens.
>
> .  .  .
>
> I dream that I am here
> manacled in this cell,
> and I dreamed I saw myself
> before, much better off.
> What is life? A frenzy.
> What is life? An illusion,
> fiction, passing shadow,
> and the greatest good the merest dot,
> for all of life's a dream, and dreams
> themselves are only part of dreaming.

What we do, what we become through what we do, is the substance of the dream which is our life. Moreover, he has also come to sense that the rational factors of one's consciousness are quite separate from one's irrational and unconscious life, which is the area of experience most in need of education, control, experiment, and the imposition of will, the life force. (Of course he has been formally tutored all along by Clotaldo in the tower; he has had instruction in politics, natural history, and the Catholic faith before being let out of the tower. In fact, his "education" is one of the sources of the delusion Clotaldo practices on him when he awakens in the tower at the end of Act Two.) It is at this point that one sees something of his self-educative process: from having been "wakened" by Rosaura in the tower, at the beginning, from the "dream" of life into the more advanced stage now of his consciousness of its reality as "experience"—what a man does is what he is. It is only disillusionment (*desengaño*), the wakening dream of death-in-life, the condition of being immured, stillborn, in the tower, that he has come to detest. Having accepted the dream of life, Segismundo is ready to act; he is ready to deal as a prince with the chance and irrational events of experience. He has begun to control his impulses.

In the case of King Basilio, his father, the life of impulse is more overwrought by rationalization and more protected by the majesty of his position. If Segismundo's progress toward higher consciousness is marked off by his soliloquies, Basilio's decline as a potent figure of authority is noted in his long, self-justifying speeches and by his fitful behavior in the presence of his son. We see him at first as a savant, a conscientious ruler eager to assure the peaceful transference of power on resigning the throne so that he may pursue his extraordinary studies. But then we learn that it is his intellectual pride, his boastful knowledge of the stars, which caused him to imprison his infant son as a monstrous tyrant-to-be. His uneasy curiosity to discover whether he has done the right thing initiates the action of the play, bringing the young, chained Prince Segismundo out of the tower and into the palace.

The guilt that fans these rationalizations is revealed when Basilio imputes to his son the murder of his mother in childbirth, using this excuse as the reason for accepting the adverse prophecies of the stars. There is also his over-eagerness to settle the crown on Segismundo's cousins, Astolfo and Estrella, by a gratuitous public test of Segismundo's fitness to rule. Basilio's fears and pride allow him to deny the realistic auguries of experience, proof of which is brought to bear by Segismundo's sharp arguments. But these arguments, the strongest in the play, do not overcome Basilio; the power of arms he wishes to abjure and his own compounded fears are what overcome him. When these defeat him he is ready—as one wishing "to do something, Clotaldo,/ that has long needed doing"—to give in, submit his pride and guilt to Segismundo, and kneel at his son's feet.

But if there are mythical reverberations in Segismundo's struggle toward higher consciousness, something similar subsists beneath Basilio's tremors, something that goes to the heart of the play. For it appears that what Basilio is fighting is the blind fear of the succession of life, which he has suppressed by imprisoning his son. The power he seems so eager to resign he is actually wishing to preserve by transferring it to less threatening and remoter kin. He thereby avoids the issue of its true passage and transmission to a natural heir whose identity he had kept a secret and against whom he now gathers all the other characters to conspire. He would make this conspiracy as effective as he believes he has made his boastful challenging of the auguries of heaven. The gift of life Rosaura has stirred up in Segismundo is what Basilio has all the time been zealously withholding from him. And subsequently, when Segismundo's experience teaches him how to understand the caution that "life is a dream," the Prince is ready to accede to the soldiers' invitation to rebel against his father and actively wrest the power which Basilio has been hoarding.

To do so Segismundo must first break the conspiracy which prevents him from acting, surrounded as he is, like a bull, by baiters cautioning him to accept the illusion of life as self-explanatory. It would appear that he must break out of this chain—the impediment to his credulity and manhood—in order to be disillusioned and thrown back into the nullity of dreaming before he can understand the use of power necessary to subjugate his father. Then he must use renunciation to cast off the illusion of false victory—which is the enjoyment of power for its own sake —and incidentally, to re-establish the structure of society which his rebellion has so severely threatened. All these are forces and tests which Basilio's hidden fear and intellectual pride have set in motion.

To effect these transformations Calderón employs the *gracioso* Clarín and the rebellious soldier in the final act. (He has used the palace servant for a similar purpose in the second act, when needing a violent example of a substitute sacrifice. There Segismundo had to be shown as unbearably vexed by the conspiracy he had not yet been able to withstand; he could not yet strike out against any person greater than the presumptuous servant and succeed.) Another heedless and arbitrary aspect of power manipulation, especially when enforced by rebellion, is shown through Clarín. Because he babbles too much Clarín is imprisoned in the tower and there mistaken for the Prince by the rebels. Earlier, in the second act, the Prince had impulsively taken Clarín as an ally: "You're the only one who pleases me/ in this brave new world of moribunds." Clarín is incapable of illusion or disillusionment; he stands outside the course of events in order to comment on them from a nonmoral point of view. But in the third act it is just such a point of view which Calderón finds especially useful: first, for underscoring the folly and taint of the power drive, and second, for providing a victim for another substitute sacrifice, one that must now be made for Segismundo's taboo crime of a son overcoming a father, and worse, overcoming him as the divinely appointed king in an act of rebellion.

So Clarín's fate—he is shot to death while hiding from the battle—accomplishes two things. It shocks King Basilio into understanding his own vainglory in opposing the designs of heaven, hence preparing him to succumb to Segismundo; it also releases Segismundo from the crime of rebellion. And when the dissident soldier is sent to the tower, we recognize that the order of constituted authority has been restored by Segismundo. Chaos and anarchy have been consigned to the house of illusion, sleep, and death. The tower itself is preserved; it is not destroyed. What Segismundo suffered in it others will continue to suffer. Segismundo himself points to this condition in the closing words of the play:

> Why are you surprised? What's there
> to wonder at, if my master in this
> was a dream, and I still tremble
> at the thought that I may waken
> and find myself again locked in a cell?
> Even if this should not happen,
> it would be enough to dream it,
> since that's the way I've come to know
> that all of human happiness
> must like a dream come to an end.

This speech follows exclamations of praise for Segismundo's "judgment," "changed disposition," "prudence," and "discretion." In a sense the burden of his reply to these praise words must be taken as half-bitter, half-jocose. For he has learned, among other things, that human beings are finally not as good as they may be. Their failures are significant since it is precisely these failures which cause others trouble and suffering. And under failures one would include all the deceptive ideals, false hopes, and easy disillusionment. But despite this disquieting discovery, he has also learned that life must be lived honorably, even if it does turn out that life is a dream, something we pass through dreaming. For life is also an unbroken chain, a succession of generations tied to one another, physically and spiritually. And it is also in some sense a sacred mystery that must not be destroyed. Segismundo touches on this subject in some cautionary lines in his last long speech:

> Those who lie
> and are mistaken are such men
> who'd use them to bad purpose trying
> to penetrate the mystery
> so as to possess it totally.

Stressing the nature of the play as a waking dream vision —with the leading thematic concern it expresses for the triumph of consciousness—indicates how Calderón essentializes thought and action while giving both the widest possible applicability in a strict dramatic form. Though *Life Is a Dream* is Calderón's best-known play, it is not, like his *auto* of the same title, a religious but a metaphysical drama. Yet it shares with a good many of his plays a basically anti-authoritarian bias. What is more, it is aligned with such a variety of other plays as *Devotion to the Cross, The Wonder-Working Magician, The Mayor of Zalamea,* and *The Phantom Lady* by its persistent exploration of the humane virtues of clemency, love, and magnanimity, held up against the combative principle of the strict honor code —the power drive, vengeance, absolute law. In *Life Is a Dream,* perhaps uniquely among Calderón's plays, a metaphysical problem is supported not by appeals to faith or insistence on ideality but by the proofs of experience itself. For the virtue of magnanimity to emerge in Segismundo it must be shown to overcome the lesser virtues which breed the brutalization of experience—false pride, rape, murder, and perverted sexuality. By implication the play is a criticism of inflexible rule, of self-deceptive authoritarianism masquerading as benevolent justice.

Appropriate to such criticism are Calderón's disclosures of the life of impulse which underlies the motivations of his characters. Such disclosures often lead typically to a formula whereby compulsive action, moral desperation, and distraught behavior must issue from sidetracked and guilty consciences: the pursuit of vengeance and the expression of doubt from the fear of infidelity, perverted love, and incest. But from this and other examples of his psychological realism we see that Calderón at his best is never merely a preacher or an upholder of an abstract morality. He essentializes in order to identify; he dramatizes in order to characterize; and he particularizes experience in order to show that relation of misguided motives to the espousing of false ideals and the necessity of earned perception for the attainment of practicable ideals. This still seems a lesson worth having.

EDWIN HONIG

# Life Is a Dream

# Dramatis Personae

**BASILIO,** *King of Poland*
**SEGISMUNDO,** *Prince*
**ASTOLFO,** *Duke of Muscovy*
**CLOTALDO,** *old man*
**CLARÍN,** *clownish servant*
**ESTRELLA,** *Princess*
**ROSAURA,** *lady*
**SOLDIERS**
**GUARDS**
**MUSICIANS**
**RETINUE**
**SERVANTS**
**LADIES**

*The setting of the play is the Polish court, a fortress tower nearby, and an open battlefield.*

# Act One

## Scene I

*(On one side, mountain crags; on the other, a tower, with* SEGISMUNDO'S *cell at the base. The door, facing the audience, is half open. The action begins at dusk.* ROSAURA *enters, dressed as a man, at the top of a crag and descends to level ground;* CLARÍN *enters behind her.)*

ROSAURA

Where have you thrown me, mad horse,
half griffin? You rage like a storm,
then flicker like lightning
outspeeding light, off in a flash
like a fish without scales,
or a white featherless bird
in headlong flight. Beast, there's not
one natural instinct in you—
tearing your mouth to hurl
and drag yourself through
this labyrinth of tangled rocks!
So stick to these heights like
that fallen sun-driver Phaëthon,
and be a hero to all
the wild animals, while I,
desperate and blind, scramble down
these rugged, twisting, barren crags
where there is no way but what the laws
of destiny set down for me,
here where the wrinkled cliffs

3

glower at the sun. Poland,
you greet this stranger harshly,
writing her entry in blood
on your sands; she hardly arrives
before hardship arrives.
Look where I am—doesn't this prove it?
But when was pity ever showered
on anyone in misery?

CLARÍN

Say any two, including me.
Misery needs company.
Besides, if it was the two of us
who left our country searching
for adventure, surely
the same two arrived here,
hard luck, crazy falls down crags
and all; so why shouldn't I complain,
if in sharing all the pain,
I don't get half the credit?

ROSAURA

I fail to mention you
in my complaints, Clarín,
because I do not like
depriving you of the right
and consolation to voice your own.
As some philosopher has put it,
there's so much satisfaction
in complaining that troubles
should be cultivated
so we may complain of them.

CLARÍN

Philosopher? He was
a drunken old graybeard.
Someone should have whacked him good and hard
to give him something to complain of.
Well, madame, what are we to do now,

alone and stranded without a horse,
at this late hour on a barren slope,
just as the sun is setting?

ROSAURA

Who'd imagine such strange things
could happen? But if my eyes
do not deceive me and this is not
a fantasy, a trick
of failing daylight, I seem to see
a building there.

CLARÍN

My hopes deceive me,
or else I see what you see.

ROSAURA

Standing there amid huge bare rocks,
there's a crude fortress tower, so small
it barely reaches daylight,
and so roughly made among
so many crags and boulders that when
the dying sunlight touches it,
it looks like just another rock
fallen down the mountain side.

CLARÍN

Let's move closer, madame.
We've stared enough; it's better letting
them who live there exercise
their hospitality.

ROSAURA

The front door
stands open to . . . what is it,
a mausoleum? And pitch darkness
comes crawling out as though
the night itself were born inside.

(*The sound of chains is heard.*)

CLARÍN

Good Heavens, what's that I hear?

5

ROSAURA

    I'm a solid block of ice and fire!

CLARÍN

    It's just a bit of rattling chain.
    Destroy me if it's not the ghost
    of a galley slave. Would I
    be so scared otherwise?

SEGISMUNDO (*within*)

    Oh misery and wretchedness!

ROSAURA

    Whose unhappy voice was that? Now
    I've more suffering to contend with.

CLARÍN

    And I, more nightmares.

ROSAURA

                Clarín . . .

CLARÍN

    Madame . . .

ROSAURA

             This is desolating.
    Let's leave this enchanted tower.

CLARÍN

    When it comes to that, I haven't
    got the strength to run away.

ROSAURA

    Isn't that tiny light
    like someone's dying breath
    or some faintly flickering star
    whose pulsing, darting rays
    make that dark room even darker
    in its wavering glow?
    Yes, and even from here
    I can make out by its reflection
    a murky prison cell, a tomb
    for some still living carcass.
    But even more astonishing,

there's a man lying there
in heavy chains, wearing
animal skins, whose only
company is that tiny light.
So, since we cannot run away,
let's listen and find out
what his misfortunes are about.

(*The door swings open and* SEGISMUNDO *appears in the
tower light in chains, wearing animal skins.*)

SEGISMUNDO

Heavens above, I cry to you,
in misery and wretchedness,
what crime against you did I commit
by being born, to deserve
this treatment from you?—although
I understand my being born
is crime enough, and warrants
your sternest judgment, since
the greatest sin of man
is his being born at all.
But to ease my mind I only want
to know what worse offense was mine,
aside from being born, to call
for this, my greater punishment.
Are not all others born as I was?
And, if so, what freedom do they have
which I have never known?
A bird is born, fine-feathered
in all its unimagined beauty,
but scarcely does it sprout
that small bouquet of plumage
when its wings cut through the halls of air,
scorning safety in the sheltered nest.
Why should I, whose soul is greater
than a bird's, enjoy less liberty?

7

A brute is born, its hide all covered
in brightly painted motley,
which, thanks to nature's brush, is lovely
as the sky in star-strewn panoply,
till learning man's cruel need
to lunge and pounce on prey
when it becomes a monster
in a labyrinth. Then why should I,
with instincts higher than a brute's,
enjoy less liberty?
A fish is born, and never breathes,
spawned in weed and slime;
then, while still a tiny skiff of scales
it sets itself against the waves,
and twists and darts in all directions,
trying out as much immensity
as the frigid sea-womb will permit.
Why should I, with greater freedom
of the will, enjoy less liberty?
A stream is born and freely snakes
its way among the flowers;
then, while still a silvery serpent
breaking through, it makes glad music ring,
grateful for its majestic passage,
flowing into the open fields.
Why should I, with greater life
in me, enjoy less liberty?
I rise to such a pitch of anger
that I feel like Etna, volcanic;
I want to rip my chest open
and tear out pieces of my own heart.
By what law, reason, or judgment
is a man deprived of that sweet gift,
that favor so essential,
which God has granted to a stream,
a fish, a brute, a bird?

ROSAURA

    His words move me. I pity him
and am afraid.

SEGISMUNDO

               Who's been listening
to me? Is that you, Clotaldo?

CLARÍN (*aside*)

    Say yes.

ROSAURA

          Only some lost
unhappy soul among these cold rocks
who heard you in your misery.

SEGISMUNDO

    Then I'll kill you at once
so you won't know that I know
you already know my weaknesses.
You overheard me—that's enough.
For that alone, these two strong arms
of mine must tear you apart.

CLARÍN

    I'm deaf, I couldn't hear a word
you said.

ROSAURA

        I throw myself at your feet.
If you were born human,
my doing so would free me.

SEGISMUNDO

    Your voice moves and softens me,
your living presence stops me,
and your level glance confuses me.
Who are you? I know so little
of the world here in this tower,
my cradle and my tomb.
I was born here (if you can call it
being born), knowing only
this rugged desert, where I exist

9

in misery, a living corpse,
a moving skeleton.
I've  never seen or spoken to
another human being, except
the man who hears my lamentations
and has told me all I know
of earth and heaven; but even
more amazing  (and this will make you
say I am a human monster,
living in his fears and fantasies):
though I'm a beast among men,
a man among beasts, and sunk
in misery, I've studied
government, taught by the animals,
and from the birds I've learned to follow
the gentle declinations
of the stars—it is you, and you
alone, who douse the fire of my wrath,
fill my sight with wonder
and my hearing with admiration.
Each time I look at you
the vision overwhelms me
so that I yearn to look again.
My eyes must have the dropsy,
to go on drinking more and more
of what is fatal to their sight.
And yet, seeing that the vision
must be fatal, I'm dying to see more.
So let me look at you and die,
for since I have succumbed and find
that looking at you must be fatal,
I do not know what not looking
at you would mean; it would be worse
than fiercest death, madness,
rage, and overwhelming grief.
It would be life—for, as

I've had so bitterly to learn,
bringing life to one who's desperate
is the same as taking life away
from one who swims in happiness.

ROSAURA

I look at you astonished,
amazed at what I hear, not knowing
what to say to you nor what to ask.
I can only say that Heaven
must have brought me here
to be consoled, if misery
finds consolation in seeing
someone still more miserable.
They tell the story of a wise man
who one day was so poor
and miserable he had nothing
to sustain him but a few herbs
he picked up. "Can any man,"
he asked himself, "be more wretched
than I am?" Turning his head,
he found the answer where another
sage was picking up the leaves
that he had thrown away.
I was living in this world,
complaining of my troubles,
and when I asked myself the question,
"Can there be another person
whose luck is worse than mine?"
pitifully you answered me.
Now, coming to my senses,
I find that you have gathered up
my troubles and turned them into bliss.
So if by chance any
of my troubles can relieve you,
listen carefully and take your pick
among the leftovers. I am——

11

CLOTALDO (*within*)
>Cowards, or are you fast asleep!
>Is this the way you guard the tower,
>letting two people break
>into the prison . . .

ROSAURA
>                         More confusion!

SEGISMUNDO
>It's Clotaldo, my jailer.
>My troubles aren't over yet.

CLOTALDO (*within*)
>Be quick now, go capture them before
>they can defend themselves, or else
>kill them.

VOICES (*within*)
>                    Treason!

CLARÍN
>                    Oh prison guards
>who let us in here, since there's a choice,
>capturing us would be simpler now.

(CLOTALDO *enters with a pistol and the* SOLDIERS, *all wearing masks.*)

CLOTALDO
>Keep your faces covered, everyone.
>It is most important, while we're here,
>to let no one recognize us.

CLARÍN
>Here's a little masquerade!

CLOTALDO
>You there—you, who out of ignorance,
>have trespassed on this forbidden spot
>against the order of the King,
>who has decreed that no one
>dare approach the prodigy
>secluded here among these rocks—
>put down your arms and lives, or else

this pistol like a metal snake
will tear the air apart with fire,
and spit out two penetrating
shots of venom.

SEGISMUNDO

Master tyrant,
before you injure them, I'll give up
my life to these blasted chains,
where, by God, with my hands and teeth
I'd sooner tear myself apart
than let you harm them or regret
the outrage you may have done them!

CLOTALDO

What's all this bluster, Segismundo?
You know your own misfortunes
are so immense that Heaven
declared you dead before
you were even born. You know
these chains are simply a restraint
to curb your mad, proud rages.
Yes, to rein you in and stop you cold.
—Now throw him back in, and shut
the door to his narrow cell.

(*He is shut in and speaks from inside.*)

SEGISMUNDO

Heavens, you were right to take
my freedom from me. Otherwise
I'd be a giant rising up
against you, piling your jasper
mountains up on stone foundations
till I reached the top to smash
the crystal windows of the sun!

CLOTALDO

Perhaps your being kept from
doing it makes you suffer here.

ROSAURA

> Since I see how much pride offends you
> I'd be foolish not to beg you
> humbly, at your feet, to spare my life.
> Let Pity move you, sir;
> it would be bad for me
> if you happened to dislike
> Humility as much as Pride.

CLARÍN

> If neither one can move you (being
> the two stock characters we see
> traipsing on and off stage
> in the same old moralities),
> I, who can't say I stand
> for Pride or for Humility
> but for something in between,
> beg only, from where I'm standing,
> for your help and your protection.

CLOTALDO

> You there, soldier!

SOLDIER

> Sir?

CLOTALDO

> Take away
> their weapons and blindfold them; they're not
> to see how or where they're going.

ROSAURA

> Here is my sword—I can only
> yield it up to you, since you are
> in command here; it may not be
> surrendered to one of lesser rank.

CLARÍN (*to a* SOLDIER)

> Here's mine surrendering itself to
> the least of all of you—take it, man!

ROSAURA

> And if I must die, I wish you

to have this as a token
for your sympathy, a gift worthy
as its master, who once wore it
at his side. I beg you, guard it well,
for though I do not know
precisely what its secret is,
I know this golden sword
has certain special powers.
Indeed, trusting to nothing else,
I came with it to Poland,
hoping to avenge an insult.

CLOTALDO (*aside*)

My God, what's this? Old wounds
reopen, my confusion deepens.

(*aloud*)

Who gave this to you?

ROSAURA

A woman.

CLOTALDO

Her name?

ROSAURA

I swore not to reveal it.

CLOTALDO

How do you know, how can you assume
there's some secret about this sword?

ROSAURA

Because she who gave it to me said,
"Go to Poland, and use your wits,
your guile, or some ruse to bring
this sword to the attention
of the noblemen and leaders there.
For I know that one of them
will favor you and help you."
Yet since he may have died,
she did not wish to give his name.

CLOTALDO (*aside*)

Heaven help me! What's this I hear?
I still have no idea
whether all this has really happened
or is simply an illusion.
But surely it's the sword
I left behind with Violante,
promising that whoever came
wearing it would find me tender
and receptive as any father
to his son. But now, my God, what
can I do in such a quandary?
He who brings it to me as a gift
must lose his life for his doing so,
and by surrendering to me
sentences himself to death.
What a pass to come to now!
What a sad and fickle thing is fate!
Here's my son—as every sign
would indicate, including
these stirrings in my heart
which seeing him before me rouses.
It's as if my heart responded
like a bird beating its wings
that can't break out to fly away,
or like someone shut up in a house
who hears some outcry in the street
and can only look out
through a window. Now, hearing
that outcry in the street, and not
knowing what's happening, my heart
can only use these eyes of mine,
the windows it looks out of,
and through them dissolve in tears.
Heaven help me, what shall I do?
What is there to do? To take him

to the King (oh God!) is to lead him
to his death. But to hide him
is to break my oath of fealty
to the King. That I cannot do.
Between my selfish interests,
on the one hand, and my loyalty,
on the other, I'm torn apart.
But come, why do I hesitate?
Does not loyalty to the King
come before one's own life and honor?
Let loyalty prevail—let him die!
Just now he said, as I recall,
that he came here in order
to avenge himself, and a man
whose honor hasn't been avenged
is in disgrace. No, he's not
my son! He cannot be my son.
He must not have my noble blood.
But if there's really been
some accident, from which no man
is ever free—honor being
such a fragile thing, shattered by
the merest touch, tarnished by
the slightest breeze—then what choice
had he, what else could he do,
if he's really noble, but risk
everything to come here
to avenge his honor?
Yes, he is my son, he bears my blood.
It must be so, since he's so brave.
Now then, between one doubt
and another, the best recourse
would be to go and tell the King,
"Here's my son, and he must die."
But if, perhaps, the very scruple
which sustains my honor

> moves the King to mercy
> and merits having my son spared,
> then I'll help him to avenge
> the insult; but if the King
> in strictest justice should execute
> my son, than he will die
> not knowing I'm his father.

(*aloud*)

> Strangers, come with me, and do not fear
> you are alone in your misfortunes,
> for in such dilemmas,
> where life or death hangs by
> a thread, I cannot tell
> whose lot is worse—yours or mine.

(*They leave.*)

# Scene II

(*In the capital; a hall in the royal palace.* ASTOLFO *and* SOLDIERS *enter on one side; and the* PRINCESS ESTRELLA *and* LADIES IN WAITING, *on the other. Military music and intermittent salvos are heard offstage.*)

ASTOLFO

> Drums and trumpets, birds and fountains—
> each responds with its own fanfare
> to your bright rays that once were comets,
> and when joining in the same refrain
> of marveling together
> at your celestial beauty,
> some are feathery clarinets,
> others, metallic birds.
> Thus, all alike salute you, madame:
> to cannonade, you are the queen,
> to birds, their own Aurora,
> to trumpets, their Minerva,
> and to flowers, Flora.

Because your coming pales the daylight
which has banished night away,
yours is the glory of Aurora,
the peace of sweet Flora,
Minerva's martial stance,
who reign as queen of all my heart.

ESTRELLA

If what you say is measured
by any human action,
your gallant courtly phrases
are belied by all this menacing
display of arms, which I oppose,
since your lisping flattery
contradicts the sabre-rattling
that I've seen. I'll have you know
such behavior is contemptible
(deceptive, false, corrupt,
and, if you will, just beastly),
which uses honeyed words
to disguise the aim to kill.

ASTOLFO

You've been badly misinformed,
Estrella, if you doubt me
and think my words are insincere.
I beg you now to hear me out,
and judge if they make sense or not.
When Eustorgio the Third,
King of Poland, died, his heirs were
Basilio, who succeeded him,
and two daughters, of whom we are
the offspring. (I do not wish
to bore you with anything
irrelevant.) But there was Her Grace,
Clorilene, your mother—bless her,
gone to a higher kingdom
now veiled among the stars—

and she was the elder sister.
The second daughter was your aunt,
my mother, lovely Recisunda—
God rest her soul a thousand years—
and she was married in Muscovy,
where I was born. But to return now
to the other member
of the family. Basilio,
both childless and a widower,
suffering the usual decline
of age in time, is given more
to study than to women; so you
and I now both lay claim
to the throne. You insist
that being the daughter
of the elder sister gives you
the prior right; and I, that being male,
though born of the younger sister,
gives me precedence over you.
We advised the King our uncle
of our claims, and he has called us here
to judge between us—which is
the reason why we came today.
Having only this in view,
I left my estates in Muscovy
and came here not to fight with,
but to be subdued by, you.
Now may the all-knowing god of love
concur with the subjects of this land
in their prophetic wisdom.
And let such concord lead to your
becoming queen and, as my consort,
reigning over my heart's desire.
And, toward your greater honor,
as our uncle yields the crown,
may it reward you for your courage,

and its empire be my love for you!

ESTRELLA

    The least my heart can hope for
    in response to so much courtesy
    is to wish the crown were mine,
    if only that I might rejoice
    in giving it to you—
    even though my love might still suspect
    there's reason to mistrust you
    in that portrait locket which you wear
    dangling over your chest.

ASTOLFO

    I can explain it all to you
    quite easily . . . but those loud drums
(*Sound of drums.*)
    cut me off now, announcing
    the King and his council.

(KING BASILIO *enters with retinue.*)

ESTRELLA

    Wise Thales . . .

ASTOLFO

                 learnèd Euclid . . .

ESTRELLA

    You who rule . . .

ASTOLFO

                . . . you who are immersed . . .

ESTRELLA

    Among the signs . . .

ASTOLFO

                . . . among stars and zodiac . . .

ESTRELLA

    Plotting their course . . .

ASTOLFO

                . . . tracing their passage . . .

ESTRELLA

    Charting them . . .

ASTOLFO

          . . . weighing, judging them,

ESTRELLA

Permit me like ivy humbly . . .

ASTOLFO

Permit these arms, wide opened . . .

ESTRELLA

to cling around your waist.

ASTOLFO

lovingly to kiss your feet.

BASILIO

Come, niece and nephew, embrace me.
Since you so loyally respond
to my affectionate command
and come greeting me so warmly,
you may be sure you shall have nothing
to complain of—you will be treated
equally and fairly, both.
So, while I confess I'm tired
of the heavy weight of all my years,
I beg only for your silence now.
When everything is told,
my story will no doubt amaze you.
Listen to me, then, beloved niece
and nephew, noble court of Poland,
my kinsmen, vassals, friends.
You knew the world in honoring
my years of study has given me
the surname Learnèd. To counteract
oblivion, the paint brush
of Timanthes and the marbles
of Lysippus portray me throughout
the world as Basilio the Great.
As you know, the science
I pursue and love the most
is subtle mathematics,

through which I steal from time and take
from fame their slow-moving powers
to divulge more and more
of what's new to man each day.
For now, perceiving in my tables
all the novelties of centuries
to come, I triumph over time,
forcing it to bring about
the happenings I have foretold.
Those snow circles, those glass canopies
which the sun's rays illuminate
and the revolving moon cuts through,
those diamond orbits, crystal globes,
the stars adorn and the zodiac
wheels into the open—such have been
my main study all these years.
They are the books of diamond paper
bound in sapphire where Heaven writes
in separate characters
on golden lines whatever
is to be in each man's life,
whether adverse or benign.
These I read so swiftly
that only my spirit follows
their rapid traces through the sky.
God! before this skill of mine
became a commentary
in their margins, an index
to their pages, I could wish
my life itself had been the victim
of their rages, so my tragedy
were totally confined to them.
For those destined to melancholy,
their own merit is a knife-thrust,
since he whom knowledge ravages
is most apt to destroy himself!

Though I say this now, my experience
itself tells it more convincingly,
which to give you time to marvel at,
I ask again only for your silence.
By my late wife, I had
an ill-starred son, at whose birth
the heavens drained themselves of signs
and portents. Before emerging
in the lovely light of day
from the living sepulchre
of the womb (birth and death being
so much alike), time and again
between waking and delirium,
she saw a monster in human form
burst savagely out of her womb,
while she, blood-drenched, dying, gave birth
to the human viper of this age.
The prophecies were all fulfilled
(rarely if ever are
the cruelest omens proven false).
His horoscope at birth was such
that the sun, all bathed in blood,
clashed in furious combat
with the moon, the earth serving
as battleground; the two beacons
of the sky fought light to light,
if not hand to hand, for mastery.
It was the hugest, most horrible
eclipse the sun has suffered
since it wept blood at the death of Christ.
The sun sank in living flames, as though
undergoing its last paroxysm.
Skies turned black, buildings shook.
Clouds rained with stones, rivers
ran blood. So the sun in frenzy
or delirium saw the birth

of Segismundo, who giving
indication of his nature
caused his mother's death, as if
to say ferociously,
"I am a man, since I begin by
repaying good with evil."
Hastening to my studies,
I discovered everywhere I looked
that Segismundo would be
the most imprudent of men,
the cruelest prince, the most ungodly
monarch, through whom this kingdom
would be split and self-divided,
a school for treason, academy
of all vices, and he,
swept by fury and outrageous crimes,
would trample on me, and while I lay
prostrate before him (what an effort
for me to say this!), would see
this white beard on my face
become a carpet for his feet.
Who would disbelieve such danger,
especially the danger he witnessed
in his study, where self-love presides?
And so, believing that the fates
correctly prophesied
catastrophe by such dire omens,
I decided to imprison
the newborn monster and see
if human wisdom could dominate
the stars. The news went out
the child had died at birth.
Thus forewarned, I built a tower
in the crags and rocks of those mountains
where the light almost never enters,
protected by such a dense array

of cliffs and obelisks.
Edicts were imposed forbidding anyone
to trespass near the spot,
for reasons I've made clear to you.
There Segismundo lives now, poor
and wretched in captivity,
tended, seen, and spoken to,
only by Clotaldo,
his instructor in humane studies
and religious doctrine, who still is
the only witness of his sufferings.
Now here are three things to consider:
first, that my respect for you is such
that I would spare you from servitude
and the oppression of a despot.
No ruler that's benevolent
would let his subjects and his realm
fall into such jeopardy.
Second, it must be decided
if depriving my own flesh and blood
of rights sanctioned by the laws
of man and God would be in keeping
with Christian charity.
There's no law that says that I,
wishing to restrain another
from tyranny and cruelty,
should practice them myself;
or that, if my son's a tyrant,
to prevent his committing crimes,
I may commit those crimes myself.
Now here's the third and last point—
and that's to see how much in error
I may have been in giving
easy credence to foretold events.
For though temperament impels him
to acts of violence, perhaps

they will not wholly master him;
even if the most unbending fate,
the most vicious temperament, the most
destructive planet, sway the will
in one direction, they cannot force
the will to do their bidding.
And so, having turned the matter
over so much, and weighing one
alternative after another,
I have come to a conclusion
that may shock you. Tomorrow
I will bring him here, who,
without knowing he is my son
and your King, Segismundo
(the name he's always borne),
will be seated on my throne,
under this canopy. In a word,
he will take my place here,
to govern and rule over you,
while you bow and take your oaths
of fealty to him.
In this way I accomplish
three things, each answering
to the three questions I have put.
First, if he is prudent,
wise, benign, and thus wholly
disproves the prophecy about him,
you may all enjoy in him
your native prince as King, who till now
was a courtier in the desert
and the neighbor of wild animals.
The second thing is this:
if he's cruel, proud, outrageous, wild,
running the whole gamut
of his vices, I shall then
have faithfully discharged

my obligation, for in
disposing of him I shall do so
as a king in just authority,
and his going back to prison
will not constitute an act
of cruelty but fair punishment.
And finally, if the Prince
turns out as I say, then I'll give you
(out of the love I bear you all,
my subjects) monarchs more worthy
of the crown and scepter—namely these,
my niece and nephew, who,
conjoining their claims and pledging
holy matrimony together,
will be tendered what they have deserved.
This is my command to you as King,
this is my desire as father,
this is my advice as sage,
and this, my word to you as elder.
And if what Spanish Seneca once said
is true—that a king's a slave
to his own nation—then as slave
I humbly beg this of you.

ASTOLFO

If it behooves me to reply,
who in effect have been
the most interested of parties here,
I would speak for one and all
in saying, Let Segismundo come.
His being your son is enough.

ALL

Give us our Prince, we would
beg him now to be our King.

BASILIO

My subjects, I thank you all
for your esteem and favor.

And you, my mainstays and supports,
retire to your rooms meanwhile
until we meet the Prince tomorrow.

ALL

Long live King Basilio the Great!
(*All except* BASILIO *leave with* ESTRELLA *and* ASTOLFO. *Enter* CLOTALDO, ROSAURA, *and* CLARÍN.)

CLOTALDO

Sire, may I speak with you?

BASILIO

Ah,

Clotaldo, you are very welcome.

CLOTALDO

Sire, I have always felt welcome here
before, but now I fear
some sad, contrary fate annuls
my former privilege
under law and the use of custom.

BASILIO

What's wrong?

CLOTALDO

A misfortune,

Sire, overwhelmed me out of what
appeared to be the greatest joy.

BASILIO

Tell me more.

CLOTALDO

This handsome youth

recklessly burst into the tower,
Sire, and there saw the Prince,
and he is——

BASILIO

Don't disturb yourself,

Clotaldo. If this had happened
any other day I confess
I would have been annoyed.

29

But now that I have let the secret
out, it does not matter who knows it.
See me later; there are many things
I must consult with you about,
and many things for you to do.
I warn you now, you must be
my instrument in accomplishing
the most amazing thing
the world has ever seen.
And not to have you think I blame you
for any negligence,
I pardon your prisoners.

(*He leaves.*)

CLOTALDO

Great Sire, long life to you!

(*aside*)

Heaven's improved our luck;
I'll not tell him he's my son,
since that's no longer necessary.

(*aloud*)

Strangers, you're free to go.

ROSAURA

I am in your debt eternally.

CLARÍN

And I, infernally.
What's a few letters' difference,
more or less, between two friends?

ROSAURA

To you I owe my life, sir;
and since the credit's due to you,
I am your slave forever.

CLOTALDO

It is not your life you owe me,
for a man of honor can't be said
to be alive if his honor's lost.
And if as you have told me

you've come here to avenge an insult,
I have not spared your life,
for you brought none to spare;
a life disgraced is no life at all.

(*aside*)

Now that should spur him on.

ROSAURA

Then I admit I have none,
though you have spared it for me.
Yet when I am avenged
and my honor's cleansed, with all threats
to it annulled, my life will seem
a gift worth giving you.

CLOTALDO

Take back this burnished sword
you wore; I know it will suffice,
stained with your enemy's blood,
to avenge you, for this which was
my steel . . . I mean that for a while,
the little while, I've held it . . .
has the power to avenge you.

ROSAURA

In your name I put it on again,
and on it swear to get my vengeance,
even though my enemy should be
more powerful.

CLOTALDO

Is he—by much?

ROSAURA

So much so, I may not tell you—
not that I distrust your confidence
in such important matters, but that
your sympathy and favor, which
move me so, won't be turned against me.

CLOTALDO

Telling me would only win me

further; it also would remove
the possibility of my
giving aid to your enemy.

(*aside*)

Oh, if I only knew who he is!

ROSAURA

Then, not to have you think I value
your confidence so little,
know that my adversary is
no less a personage than
Astolfo, Duke of Muscovy!

CLOTALDO (*aside*)

This could hardly be more painful.
The case is worse than I suspected.
Let us see what lies behind it.

(*aloud*)

If you were born a Muscovite,
the man who's ruler of your country
could not possibly dishonor you.
Go back to your country and give up
this burning purpose that inflames you.

ROSAURA

Though he was my Prince, I know
he could and did dishonor me.

CLOTALDO

But he couldn't; even if
he'd slapped your face, that wouldn't be
an insult.

(*aside*)

God, what next?

ROSAURA

It was
much worse than that.

CLOTALDO

Tell me,
since you cannot tell me more

than I already have imagined.

ROSAURA

Yes, I'll tell you—though I cannot say
why I regard you with such respect,
or why I venerate you so,
or why I hang upon your words
so that I hardly dare to tell you
these outer garments are deceptive,
and do not belong to me.
Consider this enigma
carefully: if I'm not the person
I appear to be, and he came here
with the view of marrying
Estrella, he could dishonor me.
There, I have said enough.

(ROSAURA *and* CLARÍN *leave*.)

CLOTALDO

Listen! Wait! Stop! What sort of maze
is this now, where reason finds no clue?
It is my honor that's at stake.
The enemy is powerful.
I'm only a subject, and she—
she's but a woman. Heavens above,
show me the way to go.
There may be none, I know,
since all I see through this abyss
is one portentous sky
covering the whole wide world.

# Act Two

## Scene I

(*A room in the palace.*)

CLOTALDO

    It's all done, just as you directed.

BASILIO

    Clotaldo, tell me what happened.

CLOTALDO

    What happened, Sire, was this.
    I brought him the pacifying drink,
    which you ordered to be made,
    a mixture of ingredients
    compounding the virtue
    of certain herbs whose great strength
    and secret power so wholly sap
    a man, they steal away
    and alienate his reason.
    Emptied of aggression, drained of all
    his faculties and powers,
    he becomes a living corpse.
    We need not question, Sire,
    if such a thing is possible.
    Experience shows it often,
    and we know that medicine
    is full of nature's secrets.
    There's no animal, plant, or stone
    without its own determined structure,

and since human malice can
uncover a thousand fatal drugs,
is it any wonder that,
when their virulence is tempered,
such drugs, instead of killing,
are merely sleep-inducing?
We can drop the question, then,
since reason and evidence both
prove the matter creditable.
And so, taking this drug with me
(actually made up of henbane,
opium, and poppies), I went down
to Segismundo's narrow cell
and talked with him a while about
those humane studies taught him
by silent nature under skies
and mountains, that holy school where
he'd learned rhetoric from birds and beasts.
To elevate his spirit further
toward the enterprise you had in mind,
I proposed the subject
of the mighty eagle and its speed,
how, in scorning the lower regions
of the wind, it rises
to the highest realms of fire
where it becomes plumed lightning
or a shooting star; and thus,
glorifying the eagle's flight,
I said, "Of course, as the king of birds,
he should take precedence over them.
That's his right." This was enough
for Segismundo, for on the subject
of royalty his discourse is full
of eager, proud ambition.
Thus moved by something in his blood
inciting him to do great things,

he replied, "So even in
the commonwealth of birds someone
requires they swear obedience.
The example comforts me
in my misery, since if I'm
anybody's subject here, that's
because I'm forced to be. On my own
I'd never bow to any man."
Seeing how the matter, so close
to his own griefs, roused his anger,
I administered the potion.
It scarcely left the glass
and touched his throat when all
his vital spirits fell asleep.
A cold sweat made its way through every
vein and member of his body,
so that if I hadn't known
it wasn't death but its counterfeit,
I would have doubted he was alive.
Then the people came whom
you'd entrusted to carry out
the experiment; they put him
in a coach and brought him here
to your chamber where all
the majesty and grandeur owing
to his person were awaiting him.
He lies there now in your bed where,
when his torpor ends, he'll be treated,
Sire, as you directed,
just as if he were yourself.
If I have fulfilled your wishes
well enough to warrant some reward,
I beg you only to tell me (pardon
this presumption) what your purpose is
in having Segismundo brought here
to the palace in this way?

BASILIO

 Clotaldo, your scruple
is justified, and I wish only
to satisfy you on it.
You know that the moving star
guiding the destiny of my son
Segismundo threatens
endless tragedy and grief.
I would like to know if the stars,
which can't be wrong and have given us
so many further signs
of his bad character,
may still mitigate or even
slightly soften their influence,
and be allayed by his valor
and discretion, since man himself
can master his own fate.
This I would like to test
by bringing him here, where
he will know he is my son
and where he can show what
his real character is like.
If he's magnanimous he'll rule;
if he's tyrannical and cruel,
back to his chains he goes.
But now you'll ask why, in order
to conduct the experiment, have I
brought him sleeping here this way.
Since I wish to give you
every satisfaction, I'll answer
every question. If he discovers
that he's my son today,
then wakes up tomorrow
to see himself again reduced
to misery in his own cell,
he'll come to know his true condition,

only to despair, for knowing who
he is would be no consolation.
So I wish to mitigate
the possibility
by making him believe
that what he saw was something
that he dreamt. In that way
two things will be tested:
first, his true character,
for when he wakes he'll act out all
he's dreamt and thought; and secondly,
his consolation, for if he has
to see himself obeyed today
and subsequently back in prison,
he'll believe that he was dreaming,
and he'll be right in thinking so,
since everyone alive on earth,
Clotaldo, is only dreaming.

CLOTALDO

There's proof enough, I think,
to make me doubt you will succeed.
But it's too late—there's no other way.
Besides, there are signs he's wakened
and is on his way here now.

BASILIO

Then I'll withdraw, as you, his tutor, stay
and guide him through this new perplexity
by telling him the truth.

CLOTALDO

You mean you give me leave
to tell it to him?

BASILIO

                    Yes, for if
he knows the truth perhaps
he'll grasp the danger facing him
and more easily overcome it.

(*He leaves;* CLARÍN *enters.*)

CLARÍN

    Four whacks I had to take
to get inside here; they were laid on
by a redheaded halberdier
showing off his livery and beard,
but I had to see what's going on.
Now, there's no box seat to be had
that gives a better view of things,
without bothering about tickets,
than the eyes and head a man carries
with him: bright though broke, he can take in
any peepshow, cool as you please.

CLOTALDO (*aside*)

    There's Clarín, that girl's servant—
My God! that girl, such a dealer
in misfortunes, bringing my disgrace
all the way from Poland!

(*aloud*)

    Tell me, Clarín, what's new?

CLARÍN

    What's new, sir, is that Rosaura,
who believes you sympathetic
to her cause of vengeance, has taken
your advice and put on again
her proper woman's clothing.

CLOTALDO

    That's good—it's right she dresses
properly.

CLARÍN

    Also, she's changed her name
and wisely made it known she is your niece,
whereby her reputation's risen
till now she's maid of honor here to
the incomparable Estrella.

CLOTALDO

> That's fine—at last I now can stand
> responsible for her honor.

CLARÍN

> Other news: with some such thing in mind,
> she now awaits the time and place
> when you can act in her behalf.

CLOTALDO

> Yes, that's the safest course.
> Only time itself will see such matters
> fully settled.

CLARÍN

> Further news:
> she's favored so, being your niece,
> she's treated like a queen, while I,
> who came with her through thick and thin,
> I am dying of hunger.
> Nobody thinks of me at all.
> They forget my name's Clarín—
> meaning trumpet—and if I once
> sound off, there's a tune will carry all
> the news there is to Astolfo,
> Estrella, and the King,
> because Clarín the trumpet
> and Clarín the man-servant
> are two things which don't keep secrets well.
> So it may be, if silence
> should ever lose its hold, out of me
> will pop some refrain like this:

> *There's nothing sweeter to the ears or eyes*
> *than waking to a trumpet at sunrise.*

CLOTALDO

> There's something in what you say.
> I'll see to it you're better treated.
> Meanwhile, you are in my service.

CLARÍN
    Yes, but here comes Segismundo.

(MUSICIANS *enter singing and with* SERVANTS *attending*
SEGISMUNDO, *who appears to be in a state of shock.*)

SEGISMUNDO
    Heavenly God, what is this?
    What's this I see, God help me!
    My wonder makes me fear it less
    than my belief, which doubts it more.
    I, in this sumptuous palace?
    I, in silks and in brocades?
    I, surrounded by swarms of servants,
    all so elegant and attentive?
    I, awake from sleep and in a bed
    of such magnificence?
    I, among so many people,
    and all eager to dress me?
    To say I'm dreaming would be untrue.
    I know quite well that I'm awake.
    I'm Segismundo, am I not?
    Heavens, tell me if I'm mistaken,
    and tell me what happened to my brain
    and my imagination
    while I slept that I should
    find myself in such a place?
    But be that as it may,
    why worry over such questions?
    Let them all serve me, come what will.
SERVANT 1 (*aside to* SERVANT 2)
    What a melancholy chap this is!
SERVANT 2
    Who wouldn't be, considering
    what's happened to him.
CLARÍN
             I wouldn't.

SERVANT 2

You speak to him, go ahead.

SERVANT 1 (*to* SEGISMUNDO)

Shall they sing again?

SEGISMUNDO

No,

I don't want them to sing again.

SERVANT 1

You were so abstracted,
I had hoped it would divert you.

SEGISMUNDO

I don't feel diverted from
my troubles with your singing voices.
When the military band
was playing, yes—I liked hearing that.

CLOTALDO

Your Majesty and Noble Highness:
let me kiss your hand and be
the first to render homage
and my obedience to you.

SEGISMUNDO (*aside*)

It's Clotaldo—but how can it be
that he who treated me
so miserably in prison
now addresses me respectfully?
What is happening to me?

CLOTALDO

In the huge bewilderment
brought on by your new situation
you'll find your reason and your
every utterance beset by doubt.
I wish, if possible, to free you
from all doubt, because, Sire, you should know
you are the Crown Prince of Poland.
If you were kept from others
and in seclusion till now,

that was due to fate's bad auguries,
foretelling numberless disasters
for this kingdom once the proud laurel
crowned your august brows. But now,
trusting that your prudence
may yet overcome the stars,
which a strong man's magnanimity
can indeed accomplish,
you were brought here to this palace
from the tower where you lived,
your spirit swathed in sleep.
My Lord the King, your father,
will come to see you, Segismundo,
and from him you'll learn the rest.

SEGISMUNDO

The rest? You infamous, vile traitor!
Now that I know who I am, what more
do I need to learn in order
to express my pride and power from
now on? How do you explain
your treason to this country,
you who hid from me, and so denied,
the rank due me by reason and law?

CLOTALDO

Alas, unhappy me!

SEGISMUNDO

You played treason with the law,
a wheedling game with the King,
and a cruel one with me.
And so the law, the King, and I,
after such monstrous misdeeds,
condemn you now to die between
these two bare hands of mine.

SERVANT 2

But, my Lord——

SEGISMUNDO

        Don't interfere now—
anybody. It's useless. By God,
if any of you get in front
of me, I'll throw you out the window!

SERVANT 2

    Run, Clotaldo.

CLOTALDO

        Alas, for you
cannot know that all this
arrogance you turn on me
is only something that you're dreaming.

(*He leaves.*)

SERVANT 2

    But you ought to know——

SEGISMUNDO

               Get out of here!

SERVANT 2

    ——that he was obeying the King.

SEGISMUNDO

    If his law's unjust, the King
is not to be obeyed.
Besides, I was the Prince.

SERVANT 2

    It's not for him to undertake
to say if any law is good or bad.

SEGISMUNDO

    I suspect something bad's
about to happen to you,
since you go on arguing with me.

CLARÍN

    The Prince is altogether right,
and you are in the wrong.

SERVANT 2

    And who asked you to talk?

CLARÍN
    I just decided to.
SEGISMUNDO
                And you,
who are you, tell me?
CLARÍN
                A meddling
snoop—I do that job best. In fact,
I'm the biggest busybody
the world has ever known.
SEGISMUNDO
    You're the only one who pleases me
in this brave new world of moribunds.
CLARÍN
    Sire, I am the greatest pleaser
of whole worlds of Segismundos.
(ASTOLFO *enters.*)
ASTOLFO
    Oh Prince and sun of Poland,
how fortunate is this day
when you appear and fill it,
from one horizon to the other,
with joyful and blessèd splendor!
For like the sun you rose to come
from deep among the mountains.
Come then, and wear the glittering crown
of laurel on your brow, and since
you put it on so late,
may it never wither there.
SEGISMUNDO
    God save you.
ASTOLFO
             Of course you do not
know me. Only that excuses you
from honoring me properly.
I am Astolfo, born Duke

45

of Muscovy and your cousin.
We are of equal rank.

SEGISMUNDO

If my "God save you" doesn't please you
and you complain and make so much
of who you are, next time you see me
I'll say, "May God *not* save you!"

SERVANT 2  *(aside to* ASTOLFO)

Your Highness should consider
he is mountain-born and -bred,
and treats everyone this way.

*(aside to* SEGISMUNDO)

Sire, Astolfo merits——

SEGISMUNDO

I couldn't stand the way he came in
and talked so pompously. Now the first
thing he does is put his hat back on.

SERVANT 1

He's a grandee.

SEGISMUNDO

And I am grander.

SERVANT 2

However that may be, it would be
better if more respect were shown
between you than among the rest.

SEGISMUNDO

And who asked for your opinion?

(ESTRELLA *enters.*)

ESTRELLA

Your Highness, Noble Sire,
you are most welcome to this throne,
which so gratefully receives you
and wishes to secure you,
notwithstanding all false omens,
and henceforth would have you
live augustly eminent,

not only for years and years
but for centuries.

SEGISMUNDO (*to* CLARÍN)

                    Now you tell me,
who is this proud beauty, this human
goddess at whose lovely feet
Heaven strews its radiance?
Who is this splendid woman?

CLARÍN

Sire, your star cousin, Estrella.

SEGISMUNDO

But more like the sun than a star.
My heart wells up to your well-wishing
my well-being, though seeing you
is the only welcome thing
I can admit today.
So having found in you a sight
more welcome than I merit,
your speech of welcome overcomes me.
Estrella, you can rise
and in your dawning fill
the brightest star with happiness.
What's there for the sun to do
if when you rise the day does too?
Come, let me kiss that hand of yours
from whose snowy cup the early breeze
imbibes its purities.

ESTRELLA

Your courtliness is more than gallant.

ASTOLFO (*aside*)

If he touches her hand,
I am lost.

SERVANT 2 (*aside*)

              I know this puts
Astolfo off. I'll try to stop it.

(*aloud*)

> Consider, Sire, it is not right
> to take such liberties,
> especially with Astolfo here . . .

SEGISMUNDO

> Haven't I already told you
> I don't care for your opinions?

SERVANT 2

> What I say is no more than right.

SEGISMUNDO

> That sort of thing infuriates me.
> Nothing's right if it goes against
> the things I want.

SERVANT 2

>                 But I heard you say,
> Sire, that one must honor and obey
> only what is right and just.

SEGISMUNDO

> You also heard me say
> I'd throw anyone off
> this balcony who gets me mad.

SERVANT 2

> Such a thing as that just can't be done
> to someone like myself.

SEGISMUNDO

>                        No?
> Well, by God, then I'll just try it.

(SEGISMUNDO *lifts him up bodily and goes out; the others follow, then return immediately.*)

ASTOLFO

> What is this I have just seen?

ESTRELLA

> Quickly, everyone. Go stop him!

(*She leaves.*)

SEGISMUNDO (*returning*)

> He fell from the balcony
> right into the sea. So, by God,

it could be done after all!

ASTOLFO

Now you should try restraining
your violent temper.
There's as much difference between
men and beasts as between living
in the wilds and in a palace.

SEGISMUNDO

Now if you get so righteous
every time you say a word,
maybe you'll find yourself
without a head to hang your hat on.

(ASTOLFO *leaves;* BASILIO *enters.*)

BASILIO

What has been going on here?

SEGISMUNDO

Nothing's going on. There was
a man who got me mad,
so I threw him off that balcony.

CLARÍN

Be careful, that's the King.

BASILIO

So your arrival here
has cost a man his life,
and on the first day too.

SEGISMUNDO

The man said it just couldn't be done,
so I did it and won the bet.

BASILIO

Prince, I am greatly grieved.
I came to see you, supposing
that, being warned against
the ascendancy of certain stars,
you were overcoming adverse fate;
but I find you in a rage instead,
and that your first act here

49

has been a heinous murder.
How can I welcome you
with open arms, knowing that yours,
so cruelly skilled, have dealt out death?
Who could view the naked knife
still dripping from its fatal thrust
and not be fearful? Who could approach
the bloody scene where another man
was killed and not find himself repelled?
From such a deed the bravest man
instinctively recoils.
So I withdraw from your embrace,
for there I see your arms
as that death-dealing instrument
still raised above the fatal scene.
I who had hoped to meet and clasp you
warmly in fond welcome
can only drop my arms,
afraid of what your own have done.

SEGISMUNDO

I can do without your fond embrace,
as I've done without it till now,
because a father who can treat me
with such uncanny cruelty,
being disposed to cast me off
so scornfully he has me
brought up like an animal,
chained up like a freak, and wanting
to see me dead—what does it matter
to me if he embraces me or not,
when he's deprived me of the right
to be a human being?

BASILIO

God in Heaven, if only
I'd never given you a life,
I'd never have to hear your voice

or look at your outrageous face.

SEGISMUNDO

If you'd never given me a life
I'd have no complaint against you,
but since you did and then
deprived me of it, I must complain.
If giving something freely
is a rare and noble thing,
to take it back again
is as base as one can be.

BASILIO

Is this the way you thank me
for making you a prince who were
a poor and lowly prisoner?

SEGISMUNDO

But what's there to thank you for?
What are you really giving me,
tyrant over my free will,
now that you've grown so old and feeble
that you're dying? Are you giving me
anything that isn't mine?
You're my father and my King.
And so all this majesty
is what justice and the law
of nature already grant me.
While this is my true station,
I am not obliged to you at all,
but could call you to account instead
for all the years you've robbed me
of liberty and life and honor.
Indeed, you have me to thank
for making no demands on you,
since it is you who are in my debt.

BASILIO

Insolent barbarian,
you've confirmed the prophecy

of Heaven, to which I now appeal
to look at you, brash and puffed up
with pride. Though now you know
the truth about yourself
and are completely undeceived,
and though you see yourself preferred
above all others, I am warning you,
be moderate and humble,
for you may find you're only dreaming
though you think yourself awake.

(*He leaves.*)

SEGISMUNDO

Can it be I'm only dreaming
though I think myself awake?
I am not dreaming, for I know
and feel what I have been
and what I am; now you may be
repentant, but that will do no good.
I know who I am, and however
you bemoan it and regret it,
you cannot rob me of the fact
that I am the born heir to this throne.
And if you once had me bound in chains,
that was because I had
no notion who I was,
but now I know exactly who I am,
and that's knowing I am
partly beast and partly man.

(ROSAURA *enters, dressed as a woman.*)

ROSAURA (*aside*)

Here I come to find Estrella,
but dreading to think that
Astolfo may find me. Clotaldo
wishes him not to know who I am
nor to catch sight of me since,
Clotaldo says, it vitally

affects my honor. And I trust
his interest now, grateful
for his support of me,
my life and honor both.

CLARÍN (*to* SEGISMUNDO)

What is it here you've liked most among
the things you've seen and wondered at?

SEGISMUNDO

Nothing has amazed me here
that I had not foreseen.
But if there were anything
in this world that may have struck me,
it's a woman's beauty.
Among the books I used to have
I once read that God put
most of His attention
into creating man,
a little world unto himself.
Instead, I think, it should have been
in His creating woman,
a little heaven unto herself,
encompassing in her a beauty
as superior to a man's
as Heaven is to earth—
and more, if she's the one
I'm gazing at this moment.

ROSAURA (*aside*)

Oh, it's the Prince—I must go back.

SEGISMUNDO

Stop, woman—listen to me!
Coming and going so fast, you push
sunrise and sunset together.
With the dawn and the dusk colliding
that way, you cut short my day.
Can I believe my eyes?

53

ROSAURA

    No more than I do mine, believing
    and disbelieving them at once.

SEGISMUNDO (*aside*)

    Her beauty—I've seen it somewhere
    before.

ROSAURA (*aside*)

          His magnificence
    and splendor I've seen before—
    chained up in a narrow cell.

SEGISMUNDO (*aside*)

    At last I've found my life!

(*aloud*)

    Woman—the most endearing word
    a man can utter—who are you?
    Though I do not know you,
    I adore you, claiming you
    on faith alone, and luckily
    I have the feeling that
    I've seen you once before.
    Who are you, lovely woman?

ROSAURA (*aside*)

    I must pretend.

(*aloud*)

          Simply
    an unhappy lady
    in Estrella's retinue.

SEGISMUNDO

    Say no such thing. Say you are the sun
    from whose fire that other star,
    Estrella, borrows its flamboyance,
    bathing in the splendor of your light.
    In the realms of fragrance,
    amid whole squadrons of flowers,
    I have seen the rose preside
    in its divinity,
    reigning over all the others

by virtue of its loveliness.
In that fine academy of mines
among the precious stones,
I have seen the admired diamond
ruling over all the rest
by virtue of its brilliance.
In the restless commonwealth of stars
I have seen the morning star
given precedence and chosen
monarch over all the others.
Amid Heaven's perfected spheres
I have seen the sun summoning
to court all its planets and,
as the clearest oracle of day,
in command above the rest.
Now if among the flowers,
precious stones, the planets, stars,
the whole zodiac itself,
only the loveliest prevail,
how is it that you serve
one of lesser beauty, you
who all in one are lovelier
than sun and stars, diamond and rose?

(CLOTALDO *appears at the curtain.*)

CLOTALDO (*aside*)

    I must do something to restrain him;
I'm responsible, after all,
I brought him up . . . But what's this now?

ROSAURA

    I esteem your favor,
but let silence fill the rhetoric
of my reply. When one finds
one's reason sluggish, Sire,
speaking best is speaking least.

SEGISMUNDO

    Stay here, you do not have to leave!
How can you persist this way

in evading what it is I mean?

ROSAURA

I must ask that permission, Sire.

SEGISMUNDO

Your leaving me abruptly
is not asking it but taking
such permission for granted.

ROSAURA

If you don't give it, I must take it.

SEGISMUNDO

You'll turn my courtesy
to impropriety; resistance
is a poison I can't swallow.

ROSAURA

But if that poison, full of rage
and hate and fury, should overcome
your patience, you still could not,
you would not dare, dishonor me.

SEGISMUNDO

I'll try it, just to see if I can—
once you make me lose the awe
I feel for your beauty, for when
a thing's impossible I find
the challenge to overcome it
irresistible; only today
I threw a man off that balcony
who said I couldn't do it.
So, just to find out if I can—what
could be simpler?—I'll let your virtue
go flying out the window.

CLOTALDO (aside)

From bad to worse—he makes
an issue of it. Lord,
what am I to do now that mad lust
threatens my honor a second time?

ROSAURA

>Then the prophecy was true
>foretelling how your tyranny
>would bring to this poor kingdom
>riots of monstrous crimes and deaths,
>treason and furious contention.
>But what's a man like you to do
>who is human in name only,
>insolent, insensitive,
>cruel, impulsive, savage,
>and tyrannical, someone
>born and bred among beasts?

SEGISMUNDO

>To keep you from insulting me
>I spoke to you gently,
>hoping that way I might win you.
>But if despite my courtesy
>you still accuse me of such things,
>then, by God, I'll give you reason to.
>All of you now, leave us!
>And lock that door behind you.
>Let no one enter.

(CLARÍN *and* SERVANTS *leave.*)

ROSAURA (*aside*)

>                    Now I'm lost.

(*aloud*)

>          Take care——

SEGISMUNDO

>                    I'm a raging brute—
>no use trying to chain me down.

CLOTALDO (*aside*)

>What a situation to be in!
>I must go out and stop him,
>though it may mean my life.

(*aloud*)

>Sire, look, be lenient——

(*He approaches.*)

SEGISMUNDO

> You've provoked me once again,
> you crazy, weak old man.
> Do my cruelty and fury
> mean so little to you?
> How did you get in here?

CLOTALDO

> This woman's cries brought me here
> to urge you to be more moderate
> if you wish to rule, and not be cruel
> because you see yourself
> the master of everything about you,
> for all this may only be a dream.

SEGISMUNDO

> Spouting that way about illusions
> makes me fighting mad! Now let's see if
> killing you is real or just a dream.

(*As* SEGISMUNDO *tries to draw his dagger,* CLOTALDO *stops him, falling to his knees.*)

CLOTALDO

> Going down upon my knees,
> I hope to save my life.

SEGISMUNDO

> Take your crazy hand off my dagger!

CLOTALDO

> I won't let go till someone comes
> to check your outrageous fury.

ROSAURA

> Oh God in Heaven!

SEGISMUNDO

> > Hands off me,
> I tell you—enemy, doddering
> old idiot, or you'll see

(*They fight.*)

> these arms of mine crushing you to death!

ROSAURA

Help, oh, come and help him!
Clotaldo is being murdered!

(*She leaves. Just as* CLOTALDO *falls to the ground,* ASTOLFO
*appears and stands between them.*)

ASTOLFO

Well, what's this, magnanimous Prince?
Is this the way to stain your keen blade,
in an old man's frozen blood?
Come, sheathe that shining knife of yours.

SEGISMUNDO

Not till it runs with your putrid blood.

ASTOLFO

Having put his life in
my protection should do him
some further good.

SEGISMUNDO

                              Your own death
will be that further good.
Now I can avenge myself
for your piquing me before,
by killing you as well.

ASTOLFO

The law justifies my fighting
royalty in self-defense.

(ASTOLFO *draws his sword and they duel.*)

CLOTALDO

Do not injure him, my lord.

(BASILIO *appears with* ESTRELLA *and retinue.*)

BASILIO

What, drawn swords in my presence?

ESTRELLA (*aside*)

There's Astolfo! I'm full
of terrible misgivings.

BASILIO

Well, what's the reason for this?

ASTOLFO

    Nothing, Sire, now that you are here.

(*They sheathe their swords.*)

SEGISMUNDO

    A great deal—even though you're here, Sire.
    I was about to kill that old man.

BASILIO

    And you had no respect
    for those white hairs?

CLOTALDO

                You see,
    they are merely mine, Sire; nothing
    of importance, you understand.

SEGISMUNDO

    Such futile nonsense—expecting me
    to honor someone's white hairs!

(*to the* KING)

    Perhaps some day you'll see your own
    become a carpet for my feet.

(*He leaves.*)

BASILIO

    And before you see that day arrive,
    back to your old sleep you'll go,
    where all that's happened to you here
    will come to seem, like all the glories
    of this world, something that you dreamed.

(*The* KING *leaves with* CLOTALDO *and* ATTENDANTS.)

ASTOLFO

    How rarely fate deceives us
    in foretelling our misfortunes,
    as certain to be right
    in predicting what is evil
    as to be wrong in predicting good.
    He'd be a fine astrologer
    whose forecasts were always negative,
    since no doubt they'd always turn out true.

In such a light, Estrella,
consider our experiences—
Segismundo's and my own,
each so different in effect.
For him the auguries foretold
violence, catastrophes,
murder, and despair, and so
his forecast was correct, since all this
is really happening.
But consider my case: when, madame,
I beheld your gaze flashing
such brilliant rays, it turned the sun
into a shade and the sky
into a passing cloud;
so fate seemed to promise great success,
quick approval, rewards,
and gains in property.
Fate in this was right, but also wrong:
right, when promising such favors,
and wrong, when in effect it deals out
nothing but disdain and scorn.

ESTRELLA

I do not doubt your gallantries
contain a certain weight of truth,
but they must be intended
for that other lady
whose portrait you were wearing
in a locket on a chain
that hung around your neck
when you came to see me.
And so, Astolfo, she alone
deserves your compliments.
Go give them to her quickly
so she may reward you,
for in the court of love,
as in the court of kings,

61

gallantries and vows of fealty
are not the way to valid titles
when they are addressed to
other ladies, other kings.

(ROSAURA *enters, standing aside and listening.*)

ROSAURA (*aside*)

Thank God I've reached the end
of my misfortunes, since witnessing
such sights as this is to fear no more.

ASTOLFO

I'll see to it that portrait
is replaced with the image
of your loveliness against my breast
When Estrella lights the way,
shadows disappear, just as stars do
when the sun itself arrives.
Let me go and get the locket now.

(*aside*)

Forgive me, beautiful Rosaura,
but when it comes to that,
both men and women are untrue
who are absent from each other.

(*He leaves.* ROSAURA *comes forward.*)

ROSAURA (*aside*)

I couldn't hear one word they said,
I was so afraid they'd see me.

ESTRELLA

Astrea!

ROSAURA

My lady.

ESTRELLA

I'm so glad it's you, since you're
the only one I can confide in.

ROSAURA

My lady, you honor me
in serving you.

62

ESTRELLA

          Astrea,
in the short time I have known you,
you've won my trust completely.
And so, knowing what you are,
I dare confide in you what I have
often kept even from myself.

ROSAURA

    I am all obedience.

ESTRELLA

Then, to tell this to you briefly:
Astolfo, my cousin—
to call him that should be enough;
what more he is you can imagine—
he and I are to be married,
if one stroke of good fortune
can do away with much that's bad.
The first day we met I was troubled
that he wore the portrait
of another woman round his neck.
I told him so politely.
Since he's so gallant and in love
with me, he's gone to get the portrait
and will bring it to me here.
His giving it to me
will embarrass me no end.
Please stay behind and when he comes,
tell him to give it to you.
I'll say nothing more than that.
Being lovely and discreet yourself,
you know what love is all about.

(*She leaves.*)

ROSAURA

Good Lord, if only I didn't!
Who is there so wise and cool
he can advise himself

on such a difficult occasion?
Is there anyone alive
so heavily weighed down
by fate's adversities,
and choked by such bleak sorrows?
What is there for me to do,
confused, perplexed, when reason
cannot guide me nor help me find
a way to any consolation?
After my first misfortune
nothing new has taken place
without additional misfortunes,
as though each one has given birth
to the next, and so on, endlessly,
like the phoenix always rising
out of one form into another,
the living out of the dead,
and always finding in its grave
a bed of warm ashes.
A wise man once said our cares
are cowards—they never come alone.
I say they're more like heroes—
always marching on ahead
and never looking once behind them.
Anyone who's had to bear them
knows he can do anything;
knowing they will never leave him,
he is always fearless.
I can say this since, whatever else
has happened to me all my life,
they've never stopped dogging me,
and they never will grow tired
till they see me, destroyed by fate,
fall into the arms of death.
Good God, what am I to do now?
If I say who I am,

I offend Clotaldo,
whom I must loyally support
since he saved my life; and he tells me
to wait silently until
my honor has been satisfied.
But if I do not tell Astolfo
who I am, and he finds out,
how can I continue this pretense?
For though my voice, my tongue, my eyes
deny it, my heart will tell him
that I lie. What shall I do?
But what's the use of planning to do
this or that when it's obvious
the more I do to prevent it,
the more I plan and mull it over,
when the time comes, my own grief
will blurt the secret out, since no one
can rise above his sorrows.
Since my soul won't dare decide
what I must do, let there be an end
to sorrow. Today my grief is over.
Goodbye to doubts and all pretense.
And meanwhile, Heaven help me.

(ASTOLFO *enters with the portrait.*)

ASTOLFO

Here, madame, is the portrait.
But . . . oh God!

ROSAURA

What's so astonishing,
Your Grace? What stops you?

ASTOLFO

Hearing you, Rosaura,
and seeing you.

ROSAURA

I, Rosaura?
Your Grace must be mistaken, thinking

65

I'm some other lady. No, I'm
Astrea; in all humility,
I do not merit such extreme
regard as your surprise reveals.

ASTOLFO

Rosaura, stop pretending,
one's heart can never lie;
although I see you as Astrea,
I love you as Rosaura.

ROSAURA

Since I cannot understand Your Grace
I don't know how to answer you.
I can only tell you
that Estrella, bright and beautiful
as Venus, has asked me to wait
for you in her stead; she asked me
to accept the portrait for her
which Your Grace would give me
(a fair enough request), and which I,
in turn, would bring to her.
This is what Estrella wishes,
and even in the slightest matters,
though it result in harm to me,
this is what Estrella wishes.

ASTOLFO

Try as you will, Rosaura,
you are no good at pretending!
Tell your eyes to harmonize
with the music of your voice.
Otherwise they grow discordant
and throw their instrument out of tune,
trying to temper their false notes
with the truth of feeling in it.

ROSAURA

As I've said, I'm waiting
only for the portrait.

ASTOLFO

      All right, then,
since you wish to carry this pretense
to its conclusion, I'll go along.
So, Astrea, go tell the Princess,
in answer to her request,
that I respect her too much to send
a mere likeness, and instead,
because I value and esteem her,
I am sending the original.
And you are to carry it with you,
since you already bear it in you,
being yourself the original.

ROSAURA

A bold man with a fixed purpose,
who bravely undertakes a mission,
then finds a substitute is offered,
even one of greater value,
would feel balked and foolish
returning without the prize
he set out to obtain.
I was asked to get the portrait;
if I bring back the original,
though it be more valuable,
my mission is not accomplished.
And so, Your Grace, give me the portrait.
I cannot return without it.

ASTOLFO

But if I don't give it to you,
how are you to get it?

ROSAURA

This way! Let go of it,
you scoundrel!
(*She tries to take it from him.*)

ASTOLFO

      Impossible!

ROSAURA

    So help me, I will not see it fall
    into another woman's hands!

ASTOLFO

    You're a real terror!

ROSAURA

                      And you're a fiend!

ASTOLFO

    Rosaura, that's enough, my dear.

ROSAURA

    Your what? You lie, you cad!

(*They struggle over the portrait.* ESTRELLA *enters.*)

ESTRELLA

    Astolfo, Astrea, what is this?

ASTOLFO (*aside*)

    It's Estrella.

ROSAURA (*aside*)

              Oh Love, grant me
    the wit to get my portrait back!

(*aloud*)

    My lady, if you like,
    I'll tell you what it's all about.

ASTOLFO (*aside to* ROSAURA)

    What are you up to now?

ROSAURA

    You directed me to wait here
    for Astolfo to request
    a portrait for you. Being alone,
    and finding my thoughts drifting
    from one thing to another,
    and having just heard you speak
    of portraits, it occurred to me
    that I happened to have my own
    here in my sleeve. I intended
    to look at it, like anyone
    alone trying to amuse himself

with little things of that sort.
It fell from my hand to the ground.
Coming in just then to give you
the portrait of some other woman,
Astolfo picked mine up, and now
is not only set against
surrendering the one
you asked for but also
wants to keep the other one.
I pleaded and protested,
but he would not give it back.
In my anger and annoyance
I tried to snatch it from him.
The one he's holding in his hand
is mine; you can tell by looking
if it isn't a likeness of me.

ESTRELLA

Let me have that portrait, Astolfo.
(*She takes it out of his hand.*)

ASTOLFO

Madame . . .

ESTRELLA

                    Yes, indeed, it's close;
the drawing doesn't do you any harm.

ROSAURA

Would you say it's me?

ESTRELLA

                              Who would doubt it?

ROSAURA

Now have him give you the other one.

ESTRELLA

Take your portrait, and go.

ROSAURA (*aside*)

          I've got it back now; let come what will.
(*She leaves.*)

ESTRELLA

    Now give me the portrait I asked for.
    Though I'll never look at it
    or talk to you again, I insist
    I won't permit you to keep it,
    having been fool enough to beg you
    for it.

ASTOLFO (*aside*)

        How do I wriggle
    out of this embarrassment?

(*aloud*)

    Beautiful Estrella,
    though I wish for nothing better
    than to serve you obediently,
    I cannot possibly give up
    the portrait you ask for, because——

ESTRELLA

    You're a villain and, as a suitor,
    beneath contempt. I don't want it now.
    If I had it, it would only
    remind me how I had to ask you
    for it.

(*She leaves.*)

ASTOLFO

        Wait, listen, look, let me say . . .
    The good Lord bless you, Rosaura!
    How, or why in the world,
    did you come to Poland now?
    Just to ruin me and yourself?

(*He leaves.*)


# Scene II

(*The Prince's cell in the tower.* SEGISMUNDO, *in chains and animal skins, as in the beginning, lies stretched out on the ground;* CLOTALDO *enters with two* SERVANTS *and* CLARÍN.)

CLOTALDO

> You can leave him here now,
> his insolent pride ending
> where it began.

A SERVANT

> I'll attach the chain
> the way it was before.

CLARÍN

> Better not wake up, Segismundo,
> and see how lost you are, your luck
> all gone, and your imaginary
> glory passing like life's shadow,
> and like death, all in a flash.

CLOTALDO

> A man who can turn phrases like that
> deserves to have a place apart,
> a room where he can go on prattling.

(*to the* SERVANTS)

> Take hold of this man and lock him up
> in that cell.

CLARÍN

> But why me?

CLOTALDO

> Because a tight prison cell
> is just the place for trumpeters
> who want to blare their secrets out.

CLARÍN

> Did I, by any chance, offer
> to kill my father? No.
> Was I the one who picked up
> little Icarus and threw him
> off the balcony? Is this a dream
> or am I only sleeping?
> What's the point of locking me up?

CLOTALDO

> Clarín, you're a trumpeter.

71

CLARÍN

    Well, then, I'll play the cornet,
    and a muted one at that; as
    an instrument it's miserable!

(*They take him away, leaving* CLOTALDO *alone.* BASILIO *enters, masked.*)

BASILIO

    Clotaldo.

CLOTALDO

          Sire! Is it
    Your Majesty coming here this way?

BASILIO

    Alas, foolish curiosity
    brought me here like this
    to see what's happening
    to Segismundo.

CLOTALDO

        See him
    lying there in complete abjection.

BASILIO

    Unhappy Prince—oh, the fatal hour
    you were born! You may wake him now,
    his energies and manhood sapped
    by the opium he drank.

CLOTALDO

    Sire, he's restless and talking
    to himself.

BASILIO

          What can he be dreaming
    now? Let's listen to what he says.

SEGISMUNDO (*in his sleep*)

    A just prince must punish tyrants.
    Clotaldo must be put to death,
    and my father kiss my feet.

CLOTALDO

    He's threatening to kill me.

72

BASILIO
> To insult and conquer me.

CLOTALDO
> He plans to take my life.

BASILIO
> And to humiliate me.

SEGISMUNDO (*in his sleep*)
> Once my uncontested valor
> finds its way into the vast
> theatre of this world to clinch
> its vengeance, they'll all see
> how Prince Segismundo subjugates
> his father.

(*waking*)
> But, good Lord,
> what's this? Where am I now?

BASILIO (*to* CLOTALDO)
> He must not see me. You know
> what's to be done. Meanwhile,
> I'll step back here and listen.

(*He withdraws.*)

SEGISMUNDO
> Is this really me? Can I be he
> who now returns to see himself
> reduced to such a state, bound up
> and clapped in chains? Oh tower,
> have you become my sepulcher?
> Yes, of course. God Almighty,
> what things have I been dreaming!

CLOTALDO (*aside*)
> That's my cue to play illusionist.

SEGISMUNDO
> Is it time for me to waken now?

CLOTALDO
> Yes, it's time for you to waken.
> Or would you spend the whole day sleeping?

73

Have you been awake at all
since I began that disquisition
on the eagle? Were you left behind
while I was following its slow flight?

SEGISMUNDO

Yes, nor have I wakened yet,
Clotaldo, for if I grasp
your meaning, I must be still asleep.
In that I can't be much mistaken,
for if what I felt and saw so clear
was something that I dreamt,
then what I'm looking at this moment
would be unreal; so since I now
can see I'm fast asleep, it shouldn't
be surprising that when
I am unconscious I dream
that I'm awake.

CLOTALDO

Tell me what you dreamt.

SEGISMUNDO

If I thought it was a dream
I'd never tell you what I dreamt.
But what I saw, Clotaldo—
yes, I'll tell you that. I woke,
I saw myself lying in a bed
—oh, the warmly sinister
deception of it all!—as in
some flower bed the spring shoots
through and through with luscious colors.
And gathered there around me
were a thousand noblemen
bowing and calling me their Prince.
What they offered me were jewels
and costumes rich and elegant.
Then you yourself appeared,
and changed my quiet numbness into

74

an ecstasy by telling me
(never mind what I look like now)
that I was the Prince of Poland.

CLOTALDO

Surely you rewarded me
for bringing you such news.

SEGISMUNDO

Just the opposite. In a rage
I tried to kill you twice
for being such a traitor.

CLOTALDO

Did I deserve the punishment?

SEGISMUNDO

I was lord and master there—
of everybody. And I took
revenge on all of them,
except for a woman that I loved . . .
I know that that was true, for
it's the only thing that stays with me.
All the rest has disappeared.

(*The* KING *leaves.*)

CLOTALDO (*aside*)

The King was moved by what he heard,
and went away.

(*aloud*)

So much talk
about eagles put you to sleep
and made you dream of empire. Still
it would be better, Segismundo,
if you could dream, instead,
of honoring the one
who took such pains to bring you up;
for even in a dream, remember,
it's still worth doing what is right.

(*He leaves.*)

SEGISMUNDO

True enough. And so, put down
the beast in us, its avidity
and mad ambition, since we may
just happen to dream again,
as we surely will, for the world
we live in is so curious
that to live is but to dream.
And all that's happened to me tells me
that while he lives man dreams
what he is until he wakens.
The king dreams he's a king,
and so he lives with this illusion,
making rules, putting things in order,
governing, while all the praise
he's showered with is only lent him,
written on the wind, and by death,
his everlasting sorrow,
transformed to dust and ashes.
Who would ever dare to reign,
knowing he must wake into
the dream of death? The rich man
dreams he's wealthy with all the cares
it brings him. The poor man dreams
he's suffering his misery
and poverty. The fellow
who improves his lot is dreaming,
and the man who toils and only
hopes to, is dreaming too.
And dreaming too, the man
who injures and offends.
And so, in this world, finally,
each man dreams the thing he is,
though no one sees it so.
I dream that I am here
manacled in this cell,

and I dreamed I saw myself
before, much better off.
What is life? A frenzy.
What is life? An illusion,
fiction, passing shadow,
and the greatest good the merest dot,
for all of life's a dream, and dreams
themselves are only part of dreaming.

# Act Three

## Scene I

(*In the tower.*)

CLARÍN

    I'm kept a prisoner
in an enchanted tower
because of what I know.
What will they do to me
because of what I do not know,
since they're so quick to do away
with me for what I do know? To think
a man like me should have to die
of hunger and stay alive!
Of course, I'm sorry for myself.
They'll all say, "You're right to be,"
and they're surely right to say so,
because this silence doesn't jibe
with the name I've got, Clarín.
I just can't keep still, you see.
Who's here to keep me company?
To tell the truth—spiders and rats . . .
Oh, the dear little twitterers!
and my poor head still stuffed
with those nightmares I had last night—
there were a thousand oboes, trumpets,
and what have you, playing to
long processionals of flagellants

and crosses; some staggering up,
others toppling down, still others
fainting at the sight of blood.
As for me, I'm fainting out of
hunger, because I told the truth.
I find I'm in prison where all day
I'm taught the philosophic text
of No-eateries, and all night,
the stuff of No-dineries.
If silence is ever canonized
in a new calendar,
Saint Secrecy should be
my patron saint because
I celebrate his day,
not by feasting but by fasting.
Still, I deserve this punishment
because instead of blabbing, I shut
my mouth, which for a servant
is the greatest sacrilege.

(*The sound of bugles, drums, and voices outside.*)

SOLDIER 1 (*offstage*)

Here's the tower where they put him.
Knock the door down, everyone,
and let's go in.

CLARÍN

           Good Heavens,
it's clear they're looking for me,
since they say I'm in here.
What do they want of me?

SOLDIER 1

               Now go in.

(*Several* SOLDIERS *enter.*)

SOLDIER 2

Here he is.

CLARÍN

          Here he isn't.

ALL SOLDIERS

                  Sire . . .

CLARÍN *(aside)*

    Are they drunk, or what?

SOLDIER 1

                          You are
    our Prince. We want you and won't accept
    anyone but a native ruler—
    no foreigners! We all kiss your feet.

ALL SOLDIERS

    Long live our mighty Prince!

CLARÍN *(aside)*

    Good God, they really mean it! Is it
    customary in these parts
    to grab someone every day
    and make him a prince, then
    throw him back into the tower?
    Now I see that's just what happens.
    Well, so that's the part I'll play.

SOLDIERS

    We're at your feet. Let us have them . . .

CLARÍN

    Impossible. I need my feet.
    Besides, what good's a footless prince?

SOLDIERS

    We've told your father, straight out,
    we'll recognize only you as Prince,
    and not someone from Muscovy.

CLARÍN

    You *told* my father? Oh,
    how disrespectful of you!
    Then you're nothing but riffraff.

SOLDIER 1

    But it was out of loyalty
    we said it—straight from the heart.

CLARÍN

Loyalty? If so, you're pardoned.

SOLDIER 2

Come with us and reclaim your kingdom.
Long live Segismundo!

ALL

                    Hurray,
Segismundo!

CLARÍN (*aside*)

                    So Segismundo's
the one you're after? Oh, well,
then Segismundo must be the name
they give all their fictitious princes.

(SEGISMUNDO *enters.*)

SEGISMUNDO

Who is it here that's calling
Segismundo?

CLARÍN (*aside*)

                    Well, I'll be a—
pseudo-Segismundo.

SOLDIER 1

                    Now who is
Segismundo?

SEGISMUNDO

                    I am.

SOLDIER 2 (*to* CLARÍN)

                    You pretentious idiot,
how dare you impersonate
Segismundo?

CLARÍN

                    Me, Segismundo?
I deny that! Why, you were the ones
who segismundozed me
in the first place. So you're the
pretentious idiots, not me.

SOLDIER 1

> Great Prince Segismundo,
> the standards we have brought
> are yours, though our faith's sufficient
> to acclaim you as our sovereign.
> The great King Basilio,
> your father, fearing Heaven
> would fulfill the fate
> predicting he'd fall vanquished
> at your feet, seeks to deprive you
> of your lawful right to succeed him
> and to give it to Astolfo,
> Duke of Muscovy. To achieve this,
> he has convened his council,
> but the populace, alerted now
> and knowing there's a native
> successor to the crown,
> has no wish to see a foreigner
> come here to rule over them.
> And thus, nobly scorning fate's
> ominous predictions, they've come
> to find you where you've been kept
> a prisoner so that, assisted
> by their arms, you may leave
> this tower and reclaim
> the kingly crown and scepter
> sequestered by a tyrant.
> Now come with us, for in this desert
> large bands of rebels and plebeians
> acclaim you: freedom is yours!
> It is shouting to you—listen!

VOICES (*offstage*)

> Long live Segismundo!

SEGISMUNDO

> Heavenly God, do you wish me

once again to dream of grandeur
which time must rip asunder?
Do you wish me once again
to glimpse half-lit among the shadows
that pomp and majesty
which vanish with the wind?
Do you wish me once again to taste
that disillusionment, the risks
that human power must begin with
and must forever run?
This must not, no, it must not happen!
I cannot bear to see myself
bound down again by a private fate.
Knowing as I do that life's a dream,
I say to you, be gone and leave me,
vague shadows, who now pretend
these dead senses have a voice
and body, when the truth is they are
voiceless and incorporeal.
Because I'm through with blown-up majesty,
I'm through with pompous fantasies
and with all illusions scattered
by the smallest puff of wind,
like the flowering almond tree
surrendering without the slightest
warning to the dawn's first passing breeze,
which dulls and withers the fine
rose-lit beauty of its frilly blooms.
I understand you now, yes,
I understand you and I know now
that this game's the game you play
with anyone who falls asleep.
For me, no more pretenses, no more
deceptions. My eyes are wide open.
I've learned my lesson well.
I know that life's a dream.

SOLDIER 2

    If you think we're deceiving you,
just cast your eyes up to
those mighty mountains and see
all the people waiting there
for your commands.

SEGISMUNDO

                  Yes, and this
is just the thing I saw before,
as clearly and distinctly
as I see it now, and it was all
a dream.

SOLDIER 2

        Great events, my lord,
always are foreseen this way.
That is why, perhaps, you saw them
in your dream first.

SEGISMUNDO

              You're right.
This was all foreseen; and just in case
it turns out to be true,
since life's so short, let's dream,
my soul, let's dream that dream again,
but this time knowing the pleasure's brief
from which we suddenly must waken;
knowing that much, the disillusion's
bound to be that much less.
One can make light of injuries
if one's prepared to meet them halfway.
Thus forewarned, and knowing that
however much it seems assured
all power is only lent
and must be given back to
its donor, let's dare do anything.
My subjects, I appreciate
your loyalty to me.

With my aggressiveness and skill,
I'm the one to lead you
out of servitude to foreigners.
Strike the call to arms; you'll soon have proof
of how great-hearted my valor is.
I intend to wage war against
my father, dragging whatever truth
there is out of the stars of Heaven.
I'll see him grovel at my feet . . .

(*aside*)

But if I wake before that happens,
perhaps I'd better not mention it,
especially if I don't reach that point.

ALL

Long live Segismundo!

(CLOTALDO *enters.*)

CLOTALDO

Good Lord, what's all this uproar?

SEGISMUNDO

Clotaldo.

My Lord . . .

CLOTALDO

(*aside*)

He's sure
to take his fury out on me!

CLARÍN (*aside*)

I'll bet he throws him off the cliff.

CLOTALDO

I come to lie down at your feet, Sire,
knowing I must die.

SEGISMUNDO

Get up,
little father, get up from the ground,
for you're to be my guide,
my true North Star. I entrust you
with my first efforts, aware of

85

how much I owe to your loyalty
for bringing me up. Come, embrace me.

CLOTALDO

What's that you say?

SEGISMUNDO

That I'm dreaming,
and "Even in a dream, remember,
it's still worth doing what is right."

CLOTALDO

Indeed, Sire, if doing right
is to be your motto, then surely
it should not offend you if the plea
I make now is in the same cause.
Wage war against your father?
I must tell you that I cannot serve
against my King, thus cannot help you.
I am at your feet. Kill me!

SEGISMUNDO (*aside*)

Traitor! Villain! Ingrate!
God knows, I should control myself,
I don't even know if I'm awake.

(*aloud*)

Clotaldo, your courage
is enviable, thank you.
Go now and serve the King;
we'll meet again in combat.
You, there! Strike the call to arms!

CLOTALDO

You have my deepest gratitude.

(*He leaves.*)

SEGISMUNDO

Fortune, we go to rule!
Do not wake me, if I sleep,
and if it's real, don't put me
to sleep again; but whether real
or not, to do the right thing

is all that matters. If it's true,
then for truth's sake only;
if not, then to win some friends
against the time when we awaken.
(*They leave, to the sound of drums.*)

# Scene II
(*A hall in the royal palace.* BASILIO *and* ASTOLFO *enter.*)
BASILIO

Astolfo, tell me, what prudence
could restrain a wild horse's fury?
And who could check a coursing river
flowing fast and foaming to the sea?
Can valor keep loose rock
from breaking off a mountain top?
Well, any one of these would seem
easier to achieve than putting
down an impudent, rebellious mob.
Once rumor starts up factions
you can hear the echoes breaking
far across the mountains: from one side,
*Segismundo!* and from the other,
*Astolfo!* while the throne room,
split by duplicity and horror,
becomes again the grisly stage where
urgent fate enacts its tragedies.

ASTOLFO

Then, Sire, we'll defer our happiness
and put aside the tribute
and sweet reward your hand
so generously offered me.
For if Poland, which I hope to rule,
now withholds obedience to me,
it's because I have to win it first.
Give me a horse, and let me show

my fearlessness, hurling lightning, as
I go, behind my shield of thunder.

(*He leaves.*)

BASILIO

What must be admits no remedy;
what's foreseen magnifies the peril,
impossible to cope with,
while to evade it only brings it on.
This is the circumstance, this the law
grinding on so horribly.
The risk I tried to shun meets me head on;
and I have fallen in the trap
I took such pains to sidestep.
Thus I've destroyed my country and myself.

(ESTRELLA *enters.*)

ESTRELLA

If Your Majesty in person
does not intervene to halt
this riot swelling with each
new band fighting in the streets
and squares, you'll see your kingdom
swimming in scarlet waves, and caked
in its own purpling blood.
Sorrow creeps in everywhere,
piling tragedy on misfortune
everywhere. The ear grows numb,
the eye falters witnessing
the havoc done your kingdom,
the bloody, heavyhanded blows
of sheer calamity.
The sun pulses in amazement,
the wind moves up and back perplexed;
each stone juts out to mark a grave,
each flower garlanding a tomb.
Every building has become
a towering sepulcher, every

soldier a living skeleton.

(CLOTALDO *enters*.)

CLOTALDO

> Thank God I've reached you here alive!

BASILIO

> Ah, Clotaldo, what news
> have you of Segismundo?

CLOTALDO

> A blind and monstrous mob
> poured into the tower; out of
> its recesses they plucked their Prince,
> who, when he saw himself
> a second time restored to grandeur,
> relentlessly displayed his valor
> and hoarsely swore he'd drag what truth
> there is out of the stars of Heaven.

BASILIO

> Give me my horse. Relentless too,
> I go in person to put down
> an ungrateful son; and, to defend
> my crown, will show that where knowledge failed,
> my cold steel must succeed.

(*He leaves.*)

ESTRELLA

> And at his royal side, the Sun God,
> I'll be the invincible Bellona;
> hoping to frame my name with his
> in glory, I'll stretch my wings
> and fly like Pallas Athena,
> war goddess and protector.

(*She leaves, and the call to arms is sounded;* ROSAURA *enters,
detaining* CLOTALDO.)

ROSAURA

> I know that war is everywhere,
> but though your valor beckons you

89

impatiently, listen to me first.
You well remember how I came
to Poland, poor, unhappy,
and humiliated, and how,
shielded by your valor,
I took refuge in your sympathy.
Then, alas, you ordered me
to live at court incognito
and, while I masked my jealousy,
endeavor to avoid Astolfo.
Finally, he saw me,
but though he recognized me
still persists in trampling
on my honor by going nightly
to the garden to meet Estrella.
I've taken the garden key
and can now make it possible
for you to enter there
and wipe my cares away.
So, with daring, courage, strength,
you will restore my honor,
determined as you are
to avenge me by killing him.

CLOTALDO

It's true, Rosaura, that from
the moment I met you
I was inclined—as your tears
could testify—to do all
I possibly could for you.
My first thought was to have you change
the costume you were wearing, so that
if Astolfo happened to see you,
at least he'd see you as you are,
and not think that your outraged honor
had filled you with such mad despair,
it had made you wholly licentious.

Meanwhile I tried to think of some way
to restore your honor, even though
(and this shows how much your honor
meant to me) it should involve
murdering Astolfo. But oh,
it must have been the madness
of senility in me!
I do not mean the prospect fazed me.
After all, who is he? Surely
not my King. So there I was,
about to kill him when . . . when
Segismundo tried to murder me.
And there was Astolfo, on the spot,
to save me—despite the danger,
all heart, all will, and boundless
courage! Now think of me,
touched to the soul with gratitude—
how could I kill the man who saved
my life? So here I am,
split between duty and devotion:
what I owe you, since I gave you life,
and what I owe him, who gave me life.
I don't know whom to help
nor which one of you to support:
you, to preserve what I have given,
or him, for what I have received.
In the present circumstance, my love
has no recourse at all, since I am
both the one to do the deed
and the one to suffer for it too.

ROSAURA

I'm sure I needn't tell a man
of honor that when it's nobler
to give, it's sheer abjection
to receive. Assuming that much, then,
you owe him nothing, for if

he's the one who gave you life,
as you once gave me mine, it's clear
he's forcing you, in good conscience,
to do a thing that's mean and base, and
I, a thing that's fine and generous.
By that token, he insults you,
and by it you remain obliged to me
for having given me
what you received from him.
Therefore, as giving is worthier
than taking, you must apply yourself
to the mending of my honor,
a cause far worthier than his.

CLOTALDO

While nobility lives on giving,
gratitude depends on taking
what's given. And having learned by now
how to be the giver,
I have the honor to be known
as generous; let me now be known
as well for being grateful.
That I can achieve, as I achieved
nobility, by way of being
generous again, and thereby show
I love both giving and receiving.

ROSAURA

When you granted me my life,
you told me then yourself
that to live disgraced
was not to live at all.
Therefore, I received nothing from you,
since the life your helping hand held forth
to me was not a life at all.
And if it's generosity
you admire above gratitude
(as I've heard you say), then I'm still

waiting for that gift of life
you've neglected giving me.
For the gift grows greater
when before you practice gratitude
you indulge your generosity.

CLOTALDO

You've won; first I'll be generous.
Rosaura, you will have my estate,
but live in a convent.
I've thought the matter through:
this way you'll commit yourself
to safety rather than to crime.
Surely at times like these,
with the kingdom so divided,
I could not, as a born nobleman,
add to my country's misfortunes.
In following my proposal,
I continue loyal to the crown,
generous to you, and grateful
to Astolfo. Now choose this way
which best suits you between extremes.
If I were your father, God knows
I couldn't do more for you.

ROSAURA

If you were my father,
I'd endure this insult silently.
But since you're not, I won't.

CLOTALDO

Then what do you intend to do?

ROSAURA

Kill the Duke.

CLOTALDO

A woman
who has never known her father,
and so courageous?

ROSAURA

Yes.

CLOTALDO

What inspires you?

ROSAURA

My good name.

CLOTALDO

Think of Astolfo as——

ROSAURA

The man who utterly disgraced me.

CLOTALDO

——your King and Estrella's husband.

ROSAURA

That, by God, he'll never be!

CLOTALDO

This is madness!

ROSAURA

I know it is.

CLOTALDO

Well, control it.

ROSAURA

I can't.

CLOTALDO

Then you'll lose——

ROSAURA

Yes, I know.

CLOTALDO

——your life and honor.

ROSAURA

Yes, of course.

CLOTALDO

Why? What do you want?

ROSAURA

To die.

CLOTALDO

That's sheer spite.

94

ROSAURA
No, it's honor.

CLOTALDO
It's hysteria.

ROSAURA
It's self-respect.

CLOTALDO
You're in a frenzy.

ROSAURA
Angry, outraged!

CLOTALDO
So there's no way to curb
your blind passion?

ROSAURA
No, there's not.

CLOTALDO
Who's to help you?

ROSAURA
Myself.

CLOTALDO
And no other way?

ROSAURA
No other way.

CLOTALDO
Consider now, if there's another——

ROSAURA
Another way to ruin myself, of course.
(*She leaves.*)

CLOTALDO
Daughter, wait for me—I'll go
with you, and we'll be lost together.
(*He leaves.*)

## Scene III

*(An open field.* SEGISMUNDO *in animal skins;* SOLDIERS *marching, drum beats;* CLARÍN.*)*

SEGISMUNDO

        If old Rome, in its triumphant
        Golden Age, could see me now,
        how she'd rejoice at the strange sight
        of a wild animal leading
        mighty armies, for whom,
        in his high purposes,
        the conquest of the firmament
        is but a paltry thing. And yet,
        my soul, let us not fly too high,
        or the little fame we have
        will vanish, and when I wake
        I'll plague myself for having gained
        so much only to lose it all;
        so, the less I feel attached to now,
        the easier to lose it later.

*(A bugle is sounded.)*

CLARÍN

        Mounted on a fire-eating steed
        (excuse me if I touch things up
        a bit in telling you this story),
        on whose hide a map is finely drawn,
        for of course his body is the earth,
        and his heart the fire locked up
        in his breast, his froth the sea,
        his breath the wind, and in
        this sweltering chaos I stand
        agape, since heart, froth, body, breath,
        are monsterized by fire, earth, sea, wind—
        mounted on this dappled steed,
        which feels the rider's spur

bidding it to gallop (say to fly
instead of gallop), I mean, look here,
there's a very lively woman
riding up to meet you.

SEGISMUNDO

Her light blinds me.

CLARÍN

God, it's Rosaura.

(*He withdraws.*)

SEGISMUNDO

Heaven has restored her to me.

(ROSAURA *enters in the loose blouse and wide skirts of a
peasant woman, and wearing a sword and a dagger.*)

ROSAURA

Magnanimous Segismundo,
your heroic majesty rises
with the daylight of your deed
out of your shadowy long night.
Like the sun regaining lustre
as it rises from Aurora's arms
to shine on plants and roses,
seas and mountains, gazing
golden-crowned abroad and shedding rays
that twinkle in the foam
and flash upon the summits,
so too you come now, a bright new sun
of Poland rising in the world.
Oh aid this poor unhappy woman
who lies prostrate at your feet,
and help her both because she is
a woman and is unprotected,
two reasons to obligate
any man who prides himself
on being valiant—either one
should do or be more than enough.
Three times now I've surprised you and

three times you've failed to recognize me,
because each time you saw me I was
someone else and dressed differently.
The first time you took me for a man.
That's when you were heavily confined
in prison, where your life was so
wretched that it made my own sorrows
seem trivial. The next time
you admired me as a woman,
when all the pomp of majesty
was to you a dream, a fantasy,
a fleeting shadow. The third time is
today, when I appear before you
as a monstrous hybrid:
armed for combat as a man,
but in woman's clothing.
Now to rouse your sympathy,
the better to dispose you
to my cause, hear my tragic story.
My mother was a noblewoman
in Muscovy, who, since she was
unfortunate, must have been
most beautiful. Her betrayer
saw her there, whose name I cannot tell
because I did not know him, yet know
there was something valiant in him
because the same stuff stirs in me.
Sometimes when I think he fathered me,
a perverse idea seizes me:
I'm sorry I wasn't born a pagan
so I could tell myself
he was like one of those gods
who changed himself into a shower
of gold, a swan, a bull,
on Danae, Leda, and Europa.
That's odd: I thought I'd just been

rambling on, telling old tales
of treachery, but I find
I've told you in a nutshell
how my mother was deceived
by tender love's expression,
being herself more beautiful
than any woman, but like us all,
unhappy. His promises
to marry her she took
so guilelessly that to this day
the thought of them starts her weeping.
As Aeneas did on fleeing Troy,
this scoundrel fled, leaving her his sword.
It's the same one sheathed here at my side,
which I'll bare before my story ends.
This was the loosely tied knot—
neither binding enough
for a marriage nor open
enough to punish as a crime—
out of which I myself was born,
my mother's image, not in beauty
but in bad luck and its aftermath.
I needn't stop to tell you how,
having inherited such luck,
my fate has been as grim as hers.
All I can tell you is that the man
who destroyed my honor and good name
is . . . Astolfo. Simply naming him
floods and chokes my heart with rage,
as if I'd named my worst enemy.
Astolfo was the faithless wretch
who, forgetting love's delights
(for when one's love is past, even
its memory fades away),
came here to Poland, fresh for new
conquest, to marry Estrella,

her torch lit against my setting sun.
Who'd have thought after one happy star
had brought two lovers together
that another star (Estrella)
should then rise to pull them apart?
Hurt, insulted, my sadness turned
to madness, and I froze up inside—
I mean that all of Hell's confusions
went sweeping through my head
like voices howling out
of my own Tower of Babel
I decided to be silent,
and speak my troubles wordlessly,
because there are anxieties
too painful for words and
only feelings may express.
Alone with her one day,
my mother Violante
tore wide open in my breast
the prison where these were hidden.
They came swarming out like troops tripping
over one another.
I was not ashamed to speak of them.
For, knowing that the person to whom
one confesses one's weaknesses
has herself been prone in the same way
makes the telling easier
and the burden lighter.
Sometimes there's purpose in
a bad example. And so,
as she listened to my troubles,
she was sympathetic
and tried to console me
by telling me of her own.
How easily can the judge who sinned
excuse that sin in another!

Sad experience had taught her
not to entrust the cause of honor
to lapsing time or to occasion.
She applied this lesson
to me in my unhappiness,
advising me to follow him
and, with relentless courtesy,
persuade him to restore my honor.
Also, to minimize the risks,
fate designed that I should go
disguised as a gentleman.
Mother took down this ancient sword
I wear (and the time approaches,
as I promised, to unsheathe it)
and, trusting in its power, told me,
"Go to Poland, and make sure that
those at court see you wearing this blade.
For surely someone among them
will be sympathetic to you
and defend you in your plight."
Since it's known and not worth retelling,
I'll only mention the wild horse
that threw me and left me at your cave,
where you saw me and were astonished.
We may also pass over how
Clotaldo first became my close
supporter, interceded for me,
and got the King to spare my life;
then, when Clotaldo found out
who I was, convinced me I must
change back into my own dress
and join Estrella's retinue,
where I managed rather skillfully
to block Astolfo's courtship
and his plans to marry her.
Again we can pass over details:

how you saw me there once more,
dressed as a woman, and how
confused you were by all those changes.
Let's pass on to Clotaldo.
Convinced that now the fair Estrella
and Astolfo must marry and rule,
he urged me to drop my prior claim
against the interest of my honor.
And when, oh valiant Segismundo,
I now see you, ripe for vengeance,
since Heaven permits you to break out
of your crude prison cell
where your body lay, an animal
to feeling, a rock to suffering,
and since you take up arms
against your father and your country,
I have come to help you fight.
You see me wearing both the precious
robes of Diana and the armor
of Minerva, for I'm equally
adorned in cloth and steel. And so,
brave captain, let us go together
to prevent the projected marriage,
a matter which concerns us both:
me, to keep the man who's vowed
to be my husband from marrying
another, and you, to keep them
from joining forces, whose greater strength
would make our victory doubtful.
As a woman I come hoping to win you
over to my honor's cause;
but also as a man would, I come
to swell your heart, battling for your crown.
The woman yearning for your sympathy
kneels down here at your feet;
the man who comes offering his service

lends you both his person and his sword.
But should you turn to take
the woman in me as all woman,
the man in me would kill you,
in strict defense of my good name;
for, to triumph in the war of love,
I must be both the humbled woman
who appeals to you and the man
who's out for honor and for glory.

SEGISMUNDO (*aside*)

If it's true that I'm still dreaming,
oh God, suspend my memory,
for it's impossible to crowd
so many things in one dream.
God, let me escape from all this,
or else give up thinking of it!
Who ever found himself confronting
such terrible ambiguities?
If I only dreamed the grandeur
in which I saw myself before,
how can this woman bring up details
known patently to me alone?
Then it was all true and not a dream;
but if true—which would only make things
more, not less, confusing—
how can my life be called a dream?
Are all glories like dreams—
the true ones taken to be false,
and the false ones, to be true?
There's so little difference
beween one and the other
that we cannot be sure if what
we're seeing and enjoying
is simple fact or an illusion!
Can it be the copy is so like
the original that no one knows

which is which? If this is so,
and one must be prepared to find
all pomp and majesty,
all the power and the glory,
vanishing among the shadows, then
let us learn to take advantage
of the little while that's granted us,
because all we can enjoy now
is what's to be enjoyed between dreams.
Rosaura's in my power;
my soul adores her beauty . . .
Let's take advantage of the moment.
Let love break all laws of gallantry
and the trust that lets her lie there
at my feet. It's all a dream,
and being such, let it be glad;
it'll turn sour soon enough.
My own reasoning convinces me
again, but let's see now.
If it's all a dream, all vainglory,
who'd want to substitute vanity
that's human for glory that's divine?
Is not all our former bliss a dream?
Does not a man who's known great joy
tell himself, when the thought of it
returns, "Surely it was all a dream"?
If this proves I'm disillusioned,
knowing that pleasure is a lovely flame
soon turned to ashes by the wind,
let me aim at what is lasting,
that longer-living glory
where joys are not a dream
nor greatness swallowed in a sleep.
Rosaura has lost her honor.
The duty of a prince is not
to take it but to give it back.

By God, then, I shall restore
her reputation before I claim
my crown. Meanwhile I turn my back
on her; the temptation
is more than I can bear.

(*to a* SOLDIER)

Sound the call to arms! This day
must see me fighting before darkness
buries its gold rays in dark green waves.

ROSAURA

But, Sire, is this the way you'd leave me?
Without a single word?
Doesn't my plight affect you?
Doesn't my anguish move you?
Sire, how is this possible—
you neither listen nor glance at me.
Won't you even turn and look at me?

SEGISMUNDO

Because your honor hangs by a thread,
Rosaura, I must be cruel now
in order to be kind.
Words fail me in reply
so my honor will not fail.
I do not dare to talk to you,
because my deeds must do the talking.
I do not even look at you because,
as someone sworn to look after
your honor, I have all I can do
to keep from looking at your beauty.

(*He leaves with the* SOLDIERS.)

ROSAURA

God, why all these riddles now?
After all my troubles,
to be left with piercing out
a meaning from such puzzling replies!

(CLARÍN *enters.*)

105

CLARÍN

> Madame, is it all right for me
> to see you?

ROSAURA

> Clarín! Where have you been?

CLARÍN

> Cooped up in a tower, and reading
> my fortune—life or death—in a deck
> of cards. The first card frowned at me,
> thumbs down: my life is forfeit. Poof!
> that's when I came close to bursting.

ROSAURA

> But why?

CLARÍN

> Because I know the secret
> of who you are and, in fact,
> Clotaldo . . . But what's all that noise?

(*The sound of drums.*)

ROSAURA

> What can it be?

CLARÍN

> An armed squad's left the besieged palace
> to fight and overcome
> Segismundo's wild armies.

ROSAURA

> Then how can I be such a coward
> and not be at his side
> to scandalize the world that basks in
> so much cruelty and anarchy?

(*She leaves.*)

VOICES

> Long live our invincible King!

OTHER VOICES

> Long live our liberty!

CLARÍN

> Long live both—liberty and King!

Let them live together;
I don't care what they're called
so long as I'm not called.
I'll just take French leave now
from all this ruckus and, like Nero,
not give a damn who gets it or how,
unless it's for myself.
This spot here between the rocks
looks mighty well protected
and out of the way enough for me
to watch all the fireworks.
Death won't find me here—to hell with it!

(*He hides; drum beats, the call to arms, and* BASILIO, CLO-
TALDO, ASTOLFO *enter, fleeing.*)

BASILIO

No king was ever more regretful,
no father more beset, ill-used.

CLOTALDO

Your army is beaten,
and retreating everywhere pell-mell.

ASTOLFO

The traitors are victorious.

BASILIO

In such wars the victors
are always considered loyal,
the vanquished, always traitors.
Clotaldo, let us escape the wrath
and ruthlessness of a tyrant son.

(*Shots are fired offstage;* CLARÍN *falls wounded out of his
hiding place.*)

CLARÍN

Heaven help me!

ASTOLFO

Who is
this unhappy soldier, fallen
so bloodily at your feet?

CLARÍN

    A man whose luck ran out.
    Trying to hide from death,
    I ran straight into it.
    I discovered it by fleeing it;
    for death, no place is secret.
    From this you clearly may conclude,
    the man who most avoids its sting
    is stung the quickest. Turn back, therefore—
    go back to that bloody battlefield;
    there's more safety in the midst
    of clashing arms and fire
    than in the highest mountain passes.
    And there's no safe highway leading past
    the force of destiny
    or fate's inclemency.
    So if by fleeing you now attempt
    to free yourselves from death, remember,
    you die when it's God's will you die.
(*He stumbles out and falls offstage.*)

BASILIO

    "Remember, you die when
    it's God's will you die." Good Lord,
    how convincingly this corpse
    reflects upon our error,
    showing our ignorance the way
    to greater understanding,
    and all this spoken from the mouth
    of a wound trickling out its gore,
    a bloody tongue lengthening
    with eloquence, to teach us how vain
    are men's deliberations when set
    against a higher will and cause.
    So in endeavoring to free
    my country of murder
    and sedition, I succeeded

only in giving it away
to murderers and traitors.

CLOTALDO

Although it's true, Sire, that fate
knows all the ways and byways,
and can pick its man out of a crack
between two heavy boulders,
still it isn't Christian to believe
there's nothing to pit against fate's wrath.
Because there is—a manly prudence
will conquer fate's adversities.
But since you're not yourself exempt
from such contingencies, do something
now, in order to protect yourself.

ASTOLFO

Clotaldo speaks to you, Sire,
as a man of prudence and ripe years,
and I, simply as a valiant youth.
Hidden in some nearby thickets,
there's a horse that runs like lightning.
Take it and escape, and I'll
keep you covered from behind.

BASILIO

If God intends that I should die here,
or death awaits me somewhere nearby,
I should like to meet it face to face.

(*A call to arms;* SEGISMUNDO *and the whole company enter.*)

SOLDIER

Somewhere among these twisting paths
and heavy branches, the King
is hiding.

SEGISMUNDO

            Go after him.
Comb every plant and tree,
trunk by trunk and twig by twig,
until you find him.

CLOTALDO
Sire, escape now.

BASILIO
Why?

CLOTALDO
What will you do?

BASILIO
Step aside,
Astolfo.

CLOTALDO
What have you mind?

BASILIO
To do something, Clotaldo,
that has long needed doing.

(*to* SEGISMUNDO)
If you've come to find me, Prince,
here I am now, at your feet.

(*He kneels.*)
Here's a snowy carpet for you,
made out of my white hair.
Here's my neck—stamp on it!
Here's my crown—trample on it!
Smash my honor, disgrace me,
drag down my self-respect.
Make sure you take revenge on me.
Chain and use me as your slave!
After all I've done to ward it off,
let fate receive its due, and the word
of Heaven be fulfilled at last.

SEGISMUNDO
Distinguished court of Poland,
witnesses of these astonishing
events, listen to me:
your Prince addresses you.
What's written in the stars,
on that blue tablet which

God's hand inscribes with swirling figures
and his ciphers, like so much gold
lettering on blue fields of paper—
such markings never are mistaken,
and they never lie. Those who lie
and are mistaken are such men
who'd use them to bad purpose trying
to penetrate the mystery
so as to possess it totally.
My father, at my feet here,
using as his excuse
the auguries of my foul nature,
made of me a brute, a half-
human creature, so that
even if I'd been born gentle
and sweet-tempered, despite my noble
blood and inbred magnanimity,
such bizarre treatment, such upbringing,
would have been enough to turn me
into a wild animal.
Strange, because this was what
he wanted to avoid!
If any man were told,
"One day you'll be murdered
by some inhuman monster,"
would he deliberately go
and rouse the sleeping beast?
If he were told, "That sword
you're wearing at your side
is the one that will kill you,"
wouldn't it be foolish if,
to keep this from happening,
he unsheathed his sword so as
to turn it toward his chest?
Suppose that he were told,
"Deep waters, under silvery foam,

will one day be your grave"—
it would be a pity if he
put out to sea when the waves
were curling whitecaps like
foaming silver mountains.
But this all happened to the man
who, feeling threatened by a brute,
went and woke it up; and to the man
who, fearing the sword, unsheathed it;
and to the one who, fearing waves,
churned up a storm to jump into.
And, though my rage (listen to me)
were like a sleeping beast,
my latent fury like a sword still
sheathed, my hidden violence a sea
becalmed—no vengeance nor injustice
would alter the course of fate,
but, if anything, would incite it.
And so, the man who wishes
to control his fate must use
judgment and be temperate.
He cannot keep an injury
from happening, even though
he sees it coming; though, of course,
he can mitigate the shock
by resignation, this cannot
be done till after the worst
has happened, since there's no way
to ward it off. Let this strangest
of spectacles, this most amazing
moment, this awesome, prodigious scene
serve as an example. Because
nothing better shows how,
after so much had been done
to prevent its happening,
a father and a king lies subject

at his own son's feet. For such was
Heaven's verdict and, do what he might,
he could not change it. How then can I,
with fewer white hairs, less courage,
and less knowledge, conquer fate
when he could not?
(*to the* KING)
              Rise, Sire,
and give me your hand. Now
that Heaven's disabused you
of the illusion that you knew the way
to overcome it, I offer
myself up to you. Take
your vengeance. I kneel before you.

BASILIO

My son—because your noble deed
has re-engendered you in me—
you are a prince indeed!
The laurel and the palm belong to you.
You've won the day. Your exploits crown you!

ALL

Long, long live Segismundo!

SEGISMUNDO

If my valor is destined
for great victories, the greatest
must be the one I now achieve
by conquering myself.
Astolfo, take Rosaura's hand.
You know the debt of honor due her.
I mean to see it paid her now.

ASTOLFO

Though it's true I've obligations
to her, let me point out that she
does not know who she is.
It would be base and infamous
for me to marry a woman who . . .

113

CLOTALDO

> Enough, don't say another word now.
> Rosaura is your equal
> in nobility, Astolfo,
> and I'll defend her with this sword
> on the field of honor.
> She's my daughter—and that's enough.

ASTOLFO

> What's that you say?

CLOTALDO

>                   Simply that until
> I saw her married, nobly
> and honorably, I would not
> reveal the fact. It's a long story,
> but it ends with this: she's my daughter.

ASTOLFO

> Well, if that's the case, of course
> I'll keep my word.

SEGISMUNDO

>                   And now,
> not to leave Estrella downcast,
> since she has lost this brave
> and famous prince, I offer her
> my own hand in marriage,
> with the virtues and fortune
> that go with it, and though
> they do not exceed, at least
> they equal, his. Give me your hand.

ESTRELLA

> I gain by meriting this good fortune.

SEGISMUNDO

> For Clotaldo, who served
> my father loyally,
> my gratitude waits to grant
> whatever wish he has.

SOLDIER

> If you're about to honor someone
> who treated you dishonorably,
> what about me, who incited
> this kingdom's overthrow,
> and took you out of that tower
> you were in? What'll you give me?

SEGISMUNDO

> The tower. And—so that you'll never
> leave it till you die—a constant guard.
> Once the cause of treason's past,
> there's no need to keep the traitor.

BASILIO

> Your judgment astonishes us all.

ASTOLFO

> What a changed disposition!

ROSAURA

> What prudence, what discretion!

SEGISMUNDO

> Why are you surprised? What's there
> to wonder at, if my master in this
> was a dream, and I still tremble
> at the thought that I may waken
> and find myself again locked in a cell?
> Even if this should not happen,
> it would be enough to dream it,
> since that's the way I've come to know
> that all of human happiness
> must like a dream come to an end.
> And now, to take advantage
> of the moments that remain, I'd like
> to ask your pardon for our mistakes;
> for such noble hearts as yours,
> it would be fitting to forgive them.

# Additional Readings

Abel, Lionel. "Art While Being Ruled: 'Abram Tertz,' Brecht, and Calderón," *Commentary*, XXIX (1960), 405–412. (Oblique expression of repressed values compared.)

Buchanan, Milton A. "The Presidential Address: Calderón's *Life Is a Dream*," *PMLA*, XLVII (1932), 1303–1321.

Constandse, A. L. *Le Baroque espagnol et Calderón de la Barca*. Amsterdam, 1951. (Interesting psychoanalytic study of some plays and the Baroque temper.)

Cotarelo y Mori, Emilio. *Ensayo sobre la vida y obra de don Pedro Calderón de la Barca*. Madrid, 1924. (Standard biography.)

Crocker, Lester G. "Hamlet, Don Quijote, *La vida es sueño*: The Quest for Values," *PMLA*, LXIX (1954), 278–313.

Farinelli, Arturo. *La vita è un sogno*, 2 vols. Turin, 1916. (Basic study of history of the idea and theme.)

Frutos Cortés, Eugenio. *Calderón de la Barca*. Barcelona, 1949. (Survey of life and works with excerpts from the plays.)

Goméz de la Serna, Ramón. "La vida es sueño en Calderón y Unamuno," *Cultura Universitaria* (Caracas), 40 (1953), 5–20.

Hesse, Everett W. *Calderón de la Barca*. New York, 1967. (Broad survey of eight types of Calderonian plays plus annotated bibliography.)

Olmedo, Felix G. *Las fuentes de La vida es sueño*. Madrid, 1928. (On the sources of the play.)

Palacios, Leopoldo E. "La vida es sueño," *Finisterre,* II (May 1948), 5–52.

Parker, A. A. *The Allegorical Drama of Calderón.* Oxford, 1943. (Basic study of Calderón's *autos.*)

——. "The Approach to the Spanish Drama of the Golden Age," *Diamante,* VI, Hispanic and Luso-Brazilian Councils. London, 1957. (Reprinted in *The Tulane Drama Review,* IV [1959], 42–59.) (Important theoretical prospectus.)

——. "Reflections on a New Definition of Baroque Drama," *Bulletin of Hispanic Studies,* XXX (1953), 142–151. (A new view of coherence of precept and practice.)

Reichenberger, Arnold G. "The Uniqueness of the *Comedia*," *Hispanic Review,* XXVII (1959), 303–316. (On the special conditions of the type in relation to Spanish culture.)

Rennert, H. A. *The Spanish Stage in the Time of Lope de Vega.* New York, 1909, 1963. (On staging, actors, and early theatres).

Reyes, Alfonso. *Un tema de La vida es sueño; el hombre y la naturaleza en el monologo de Segismundo.* Madrid, 1917.

——. "El enigma de Segismundo," *Ramer,* II (1945), 353–365.

Sauvage, Micheline. *Calderón: dramaturge.* Paris, 1959. (Excellent survey with illustrations.)

Sciacca, Michele F. "Verdad y sueño de *La vida es sueño* de Calderón de la Barca," *Clavileno,* 2 (March–April 1950), 1–9. (On the "reality" of Rosaura in the play.)

Sloman, Albert E. "The Structure of Calderón's *La vida es sueño*," *Modern Language Review,* XLVIII (1953), 293–300. (On the interrelationship of the two plots.)

——. *The Dramatic Craftsmanship of Calderón. His Use of Earlier Plays.* Oxford, 1958. (Masterly study of eight plays and their sources.)

Valbuena Briones, Ángel. *Perspectiva critica de los dramas de Calderón.* Madrid, 1965. (Commentaries on fifty-five plays, plus extensive bibliography of Calderón studies [1815–1964], pp. 403–421, and on *La vida es sueño,* pp. 178–189.)

Valbuena Prat, Ángel. *Calderón. Su personalidad, su arte dramático, su estilo y sus obras.* Barcelona, 1941. (Types of Calderonian theatre.)

Wardropper, Bruce. "'Apenas llega cuando llega a penas,'" *Modern Philology,* LVII (1960), 240–244. (Importance of this pun and theme of the play.)

———. "The Unconscious Mind in Calderón's *El pintor de su deshonra,*" *Hispanic Review,* XVIII (1950), 285–301. (One of the few studies stressing vital role of unconscious in Calderón.)

———, ed. *Critical Essays on the Theatre of Calderón.* New York, 1965. (Eleven essays include four on *Life Is a Dream*: 1. Wilson, E. M., "On *La vida es sueño,*" pp. 62–89; 2. Sloman, A. E., "The Structure . . ." [see entry under Sloman above], pp. 90–100; 3. Whitby, William W., "Rosaura's Role in the Structure of *La vida es sueño,*" pp. 101–113; 4. Hesse, Everett W., "Calderón's Concept of the Perfect Prince in *La vida es sueño,*" pp. 114–133.)

Wilson, E. M. "The Four Elements in the Imagery of Calderón," *Modern Language Review,* XXXI (1936), 34–37. (A basic study on this reiterative pattern in Calderón's work.)